The
East Anglian
Cottage

Trevor Yorke

COUNTRYSIDE BOOKS
NEWBURY BERKSHIRE

COUNTRYSIDE BOOKS
3 Catherine Road
Newbury
Berkshire
RG14 7NA

To view our complete range of books, please visit us at
www.countrysidebooks.co.uk

First published in 2014
Text © 2014 Trevor Yorke
Photos and illustrations © 2014 Trevor Yorke
Photo page 1 © Mark Mitchels

A CIP record for this book is available from the British Library.

ISBN 978 1 84674 328 3

Cover designed by Peter Davies, Nautilus Design
Produced by The Letterworks Ltd., Reading
Typeset by KT Designs, St Helens
Printed by Berforts Information Press, Oxford

CONTENTS

Introduction

What is it that makes the English cottage so attractive to us? Why do we aspire to own homes which are often cramped, awkward and difficult to maintain when we could live in a more convenient modern building for less money? What are the magic ingredients that make us state that we 'would love to live there'?

Despite being packed with drawings, and photographs of some of the finest examples of East Anglian cottages, this book is not intended as just a visual treat. Rather, it is meant as a practical and informative guide to both the casual observer and cottage owner alike.

For me there are five key attributes that make the English cottage an iconic building type. There is the history, not just its age and all it has been through, but the changes in its surroundings which have shaped the structure and plan. Then there are the materials it is made from. These reflect the local landscape with colours and textures that make the building feel as if it has been hewn out of the countryside rather than just planted upon it. Next are the little details which instantly make us think of cottages. These include the tiny hinged windows, rustic planked doors and little dormers peeking out of the roof. The fourth characteristic I would look for is that

the interior continues the theme of rustic simplicity and that the materials it is made from are visible, like timber beams and stone walls. The final core element of any cottage is the garden which surrounds it, with tightly packed flower beds, rustic arches, and climbers clinging to the walls to frame the building and add the necessary charm.

It is these five characteristics which have defined the structure of this book. Chapter 1 outlines the history of the region and how it shaped the cottages which are found there. Chapter 2 describes the materials the walls and roofs are made from, how they are used and the problems they may bring. The next chapter looks at the details of the building, from windows and doors to chimneys and porches, with tips on their maintenance. Chapter 4 looks inside at the appearance of the cottage in the past including details like fireplaces and flooring. The final chapter explores the land around the building, how it was used in the past and what makes an ideal cottage garden today.

This is a region blessed with a subdued landscape and vast skies which perfectly frame its distinctive cottages. It is partly geography that has created this appeal. Norfolk and Suffolk have both largely avoided the blight of the industrial age, and with no motorways or high-speed trains fewer people pass through the area. This has helped preserve buildings from the worst excesses of recent times. Unlike some other regions of England, East Anglia has few good building materials. This has resulted in creative solutions over the years, bringing a varied range of colours and textures to its cottages. It is these local characteristics and building methods over the centuries that this book sets out to explore and explain.

Trevor Yorke

Visit www.trevoryorke.co.uk for more information or follow me on facebook at trevoryorke-author

A sample of East Anglian cottages with labels highlighting some of their key features.

What is a Cottage?

What exactly is a cottage? Many people will probably think of a quaint, thatched building surrounded by a flower garden and picket fence. However, take a look through a holiday cottage brochure and you will find all manner of buildings, old and new, tiny or sprawling, some in hamlets, others in large towns. Their age can be just as varied, with rustic timber-framed Tudor houses vying with modern brick structures that stretch the definition to the limits. For the purposes of a book about regional English cottages we need to clarify the type of building we will be looking at by briefly outlining its distinctive features.

> The word cottage is derived from the Old English 'cot' or 'cote' meaning a hut. It was the home of a cotter or cottager, just one of the tiers of peasantry within the medieval feudal system. At this time any references to a cottage would relate to the small-holding, including any barns or sheds and not just the dwelling itself. From the 17th century the word cottage came to refer to a small dwelling house.

A cottage is principally a small rural property, although some will now be found in towns as earlier villages have been engulfed by urbanisation over the past 200 years. Its modest structure will typically contain one or two living rooms and the bedrooms above may be lit by small dormer windows set into the roof. In many cases the original building will have been extended over the years, so the cottage today can form quite a sizable residence. Whatever changes have been made, the cottage still needs to retain a rustic charm - weathered by time and blending with the surroundings.

Another theme this book will focus on is vernacular construction - the cottages were built using methods and materials from the local area. Until the second half of the 19th century, when the railways made it easy to use cheap mass-produced materials from distant places, the small, rural property would have been built using resources extracted from the surrounding countryside and made locally. The form and appearance of cottages were dictated by the available materials, and by the traditional methods used by local builders who passed their knowledge down through the gener-ations. Sometimes a style would remain peculiar to a small area containing just a couple of neighbouring villages.

This is clearly displayed within the villages and hamlets of Norfolk, Suffolk and the edges of Lincolnshire, Cambridgeshire and Essex which make up the distinctive landscape of East Anglia. There are few other places in the country where there is such colour and variety in cottages, from pebble encrusted buildings with bright orange pantiles to pink timber-framed houses with rustic thatched roofs. A continuing rural heritage has meant that villages are still modest in size and contain a high proportion of old cottages which have escaped excessive modernisation. Under the vast skies of these agricultural eastern counties there is a wealth of picturesque cottages waiting to be discovered and investigated. This book aims to unlock some of their secrets.

A selection of East Anglian cottages displaying the wide variety of vernacular styles described in this book. Most were built between the late 17th and the early 20th century, with a few of earlier origin. Some may display non-vernacular features such as sash windows, but on the whole they are characteristic of this region, modest in their original size and rural in aspect. Clockwise from top left: Brent Eleigh, Suffolk; Burnham Market, Norfolk; Cavendish, Suffolk; and Matlaske, Norfolk.

CHAPTER 1

The Cottage Through Time

From peasants' hovels to Arts and Crafts homes

FIG 1.1: CODDENHAM, SUFFOLK: *As is often the case the timber-framed cottages in the centre of this view were something far grander when they were built. They were originally one large house and a shop, dating from the 16th century, which sometime later was split up to form a row of cottages, the one in the foreground becoming the village post office. The original owners would be quite offended if you had referred to it as a cottage.*

E ast Anglia is an ancient kingdom, established in the early 6th century by the Anglo-Saxon north and south folk (hence Norfolk and Suffolk) who had come to control this area during the previous century. In medieval times the region became important and prosperous. Norwich was a major English city and the port provided a vital link to the Continent. Many grew wealthy through trade, agriculture and the woollen industry, and their affluence was reflected by their homes and churches. The region went through a decline in the past couple of centuries, as the lack of natural resources, especially coal, meant that industry boomed elsewhere. Canals were few, the railways arrived late and there are still no motorways crossing the area. The absence of large scale development and a dependence upon agriculture resulted in the preservation of much that existed over 200 years ago. Today, the over-whelming impression, while travelling through Norfolk and Suffolk, is of a rich rural landscape interspersed with picturesque villages filled with colourful and charming cottages.

The humble homes we see today are not simply the result of a single period of building activity, or the actions of a few powerful men. Their backgrounds are as varied as their form and appearance. Some cottages were converted from trade premises or the larger homes of wealthier villagers, while others developed piecemeal from the most humble origins. A few are the result of large scale planning. Others display the hand of a single builder. Some have parts dating back to medieval times, but most will be of Georgian or Victorian lineage. They may also have been extended many times to suit new occupants or to reflect prosperous times in the village, and there will often be signs of these improvements in their plan and

FIG 1.2: DEBENHAM, SUFFOLK: *One of the reasons why East Anglia is blessed with so many old cottages is that many of its once busy towns and villages were not overtaken by the Industrial Revolution and never grew much beyond their ancient core. Debenham was an important centre for dairy produce with a thriving market and a fashionable merchant's house. Today, it is a quiet and colourful village with streets lined by a wealth of rustic homes.*

structure. This chapter explains how the changing times in the countryside have affected the East Anglian cottage.

Medieval and Tudor

For England, the late medieval period through to the mid 16th century was a time of fluctuating fortunes. Climate change brought bad harvests in the early 1300s while the Black Death decimated the population and resulted in changes to land holding which would eventually break the feudal system. In some areas of East Anglia, in particular the north and west, villages were depopulated and turned over to sheep farming, while in the south and east small-scale farming continued. Some peasants seized their opportunity, increased their holdings and became yeoman farmers while others found themselves evicted to make way for the more profitable wool industry.

The cottage appears on documents from this period as a small-holding, lower in status than the larger properties and the manor itself, but including land so the tenant could feed his family. In some cases the lord of the manor gave permission for a cottage to be built within the village or to form part of a newly developed area like a medieval version of a modern housing estate. Sometimes a cottage could be built on a vacant plot of land, the general rule being that you had to have a fire burning in the grate by the morning after you started building for you to gain the right to stay (a statute of 1589 ended the legal right of a peasant to do this but it was not always imposed so the practice continued in

some places). The quick construction of these cottages suggests how flimsy some peasant housing from this period must have been. Peasants could not afford to pay for a builder, and supplies would have been limited to what could be gathered locally. Many cottages probably only stood for a generation or two. Most would have been a low walled, single-storey structure with one room for the family to eat and sleep in. In some there was another space for

FIG 1.3: NEW BUCKENDEN, NORFOLK: *Although this seems like a village today it is in fact a medieval planned town, created as a commercial venture in the 12th century to help finance a new castle. Like many East Anglian settlements it never expanded far beyond its ancient bounds. Its numerous houses and cottages often have 18th and 19th-century brick fronts. These were commonly used to cover older timber-framed walls when a complete rebuild was beyond the pocket of the owners. This colourful row of cottages is set back from the main street and has avoided fashionable makeovers.*

livestock, all under the same thatched roof.

None of the peasant cottages from that period survive today. All you might find are raised platforms resulting from generations of rebuilding, and a layer of mud from the walls showing where they once stood. Houses from the late medieval period, which we today would call a cottage, would usually have been home to someone of high status in the community and would have been of superior quality to the surrounding hovels when built.

During the 16th and 17th centuries most villages in East Anglia bore witness to significant changes. Yeomen and peasants reorganised their strips of land into new consolidated farms. Rather than owing services to the lord of the manor in return for certain

rights, they now became his tenants. The more successful of these tenants enlarged their holding, often amalgamating with others - a process of enclosure by agreement which in many parts of the region left only the common land to be divided up by Parliament. Old manor houses were relegated to the status of farmhouse, and many of these were, in turn, subdivided to provide cheap housing for labourers. Timber-framed cottages are often part of a larger single property that was converted at a later date, sometimes when new farms became established outside of the old village centre.

FIG 1.5: FLEGGBURGH, NORFOLK:
The earliest true cottages which survive in East Anglia today usually date from the 17th century, as in this isolated example on the edge of Filby Broad. Many of them were built for specific tradesmen and specialist jobs rather than just peasant labourers. The ones which retain something of their original form are often associated with those who worked the waters and marshes, cutting reeds and manning the mills and pumps.

FIG 1.4: *An old timber-framed house from the 15th or 16th century which has later been split up to form three cottages.*

These social changes, and a general increase in wealth from the mid 16th century, resulted in widespread rebuilding of houses and cottages. The period when this happened in any particular area would depend upon acts of enclosure, a successful new local industry and the cooperation of the main landowners. Neighbouring villages may have witnessed change at different times. These new, more permanent cottages were still small in size, usually with only one or two ground floor rooms. Some of these survive today as the core of larger homes. By the end of this period the cottage had become more clearly defined as a humble dwelling, and not only for agricultural labourers but also for those who worked in other rural industries. It is from the 17th century that the oldest, purpose-built cottages are likely to date.

Georgian and Victorian Cottages

It is also likely that the majority of cottages we see in East Anglia today date from the 18th and 19th centuries. It is often forgotten that this period of industrial upheaval created just as much change in rural areas as in towns, with agriculture rapidly developing to feed the growing population, and country estates expanding. Some labourers were tied to a farm or estate and occupied the same cottage for most of their life, others had to seek seasonal employment and rent a home sometimes miles from where they worked. The loss of small fields and common land made it harder for them

FIG 1.6: COSTESSEY, NORFOLK:
From the second half of the 18th century many architects and their aristocratic clients became fascinated by the relationship between dramatic landscapes and ruined buildings. This picturesque movement promoted the use of materials in their natural form, with irregular plans and distressed finishes, as rustic old cottages became models for the design of estate workers' houses. Pattern books were produced with designs in a variety of styles intended to complement a gentleman's country residence. One of the most distinctive of these was Cottage Orne, with deeply overhanging thatched roofs, circular plans and rustic tree trunks used as columns. This example from Costessey, near Norwich, has tree trunks forming the vertical divisions of its round walls and Gothic-style windows. The construction of cottages like this was not usually through the benevolence of the rich, rather they were whimsical creations to enliven the approach to the large house. At Old Warden in Hertfordshire the workers were even made to dress up in period costumes when guests were expected.

to keep livestock or grow crops to sell. As a result incomes were supplemented by women and children who laboured in the fields or carried out a craft from home. To make matters worse, fortunes in agriculture were always fluctuating and the woollen industry rapidly declined in the early 19th century with competition from mills in the north. With little security and lower pay than their counterparts in the industrial slums, the rural labourer and his family

FIG 1.7: *Many cottages in East Anglia were built either during the late 18th-century agricultural boom or in the golden years of 1840-75. Earlier types usually had dormer windows in the attic bedrooms (left) while later 19th-century cottages might have two full storeys (right). They could have fashionable details like sash windows but were largely vernacular with materials from the local area. They were often erected by employers or speculators and were almost never owned by the occupants.*

had to live in appalling conditions even into the early 20th century. Richard Heath in his book *The English Peasant* quoted an 1867 report on the health of the poor: 'the majority of cottages are deficient in almost every respect of decency: poor sanitation, too few bedrooms, draughty, poor water supply and in disrepair'. The situation became worse as bad harvests and competition from abroad caused depression across many sectors of the agricultural industry, resulting in the poor cottager only becoming poorer.

Ironically, it was at this point that artists and architects became interested in rural houses. Paintings of rustic cottages became fashionable. They represented an idealised rural past which had a strong appeal in this rapidly industrialising age but at the same time recorded the dilapidated state many of them were in. Behind the charming imagery were leaking roofs, crumbling damp walls and worn out windows and doors. Few had services like drainage, water or gas that the urbanites who snapped up the paintings were enjoying. Many of these same rural buildings inspired a new generation of architects who sought to combine the traditional building methods with the requirements of a modern home. These Arts and Crafts designers created sprawling suburban houses with sweeping roofs and rows of low windows which set the fashion for a cottage style which would dominate housing estates in the first half of the 20th century.

At the same time landowners and local authorities began facing up to the chronic housing conditions in many parts of the country. From the 1920s, old cottages were demolished to be replaced by hygienic and spacious semis and terraces. They may have been rather charmless brick or concrete boxes set on the edge of villages but they were a vast improvement for those who had to live there. The destruction of old cottages continued into recent decades. However the potent image of their rustic charm and homely proportions, alongside the perceived peace and tranquillity of country life, appealed to the urban middle classes and during the second half of the 20th century cottages were snapped up, renovated and extended to give the

FIG 1.8: *Estate cottages such as these two 19th-century examples were a significant improvement on the hovels most labourers lived in. Nathaniel Kent in the 1770s was one of the first to recommend that landlords provide better housing for their staff, pointing out that they spent more on stables for their horses than they did on the homes of those who worked their land. His ideal cottages were still small, he stated that all they required was, 'a warm, comfortable plain room for the poor inhabitants to eat their morsel in, an oven to bake their bread, a little receptacle for their small beer and provisions, and two wholesome lodging apartments, one for the man and wife, another for the children.' Despite an attractive exterior, most estate cottages built in the late 18th and 19th century were compact and utilitarian.*

FIG 1.9: *Paintings of cottages by the Victorian artist Helen Allingham, as pictured above, captured not just their romantic element but also their poor state of repair. Crumbling walls, patchy thatch and worn out fittings could only be hidden so much by colourful flowers and climbing plants.*

■ The real Victorian cottage

Although there were some well-built cottages on country estates, the majority of labourers in the 19th century occupied homes which, despite being visually picturesque, were appalling to live in. Richard Heath used his 1893 book *The English Peasant* to catalogue the true state of cottages as found by health officials over the previous decades. He describes cottages as, 'crazy, dilapidated hovels, shaking with every wind', while inspectors described many cottages as, 'tumbledown and ruinous, not water-tight, very deficient in bedroom accommodation, and indecent sanitary arrangements'. It was often stated that bedrooms were found with children sleeping on pillows soaked wet by rain pouring in through a thatched roof and families sick with fever having to stay in the same room as a corpse. A report of dwellings in Norfolk in 1863 echoed many of the same complaints; rotten and shapeless thatched roofs full of holes and weeds, windows patched with rags, and walls cracked with up to 11 people found sleeping together in one bedroom and children sick with fever for months. This overcrowding was a particular problem in the Fens where drainage had created large fields but few villages, so farmers gathered gangs of men, women and children who had to march often over ten miles a day to and from the fields. These poor conditions were blamed for many of the social ills in rural East Anglia. It was estimated that around 10 per cent of children were illegitimate, boys and girls as young as seven had to go out to work and the use of opium in the form of penny sticks, pills or cordials was a widespread problem. Many of these hovels were so poorly built that they were simply flattened when better housing became available in the early 20th century. However, a few survive at the heart of modern cottages; their previous occupants would think they were in a palace if they could see what they looked like today.

FIG 1.10: *Terraced cottages dating from 1875 (left) and a larger pair of semis (right) which is typical of those built by local authorities for farm labourers on the edge of villages from the 1920s to 1950s. These were larger than earlier cottages and were double pile, that is with full-sized front and rear rooms.*

century-old buildings a new lease of life.

The cottage plan

The building of more permanent cottages from the 17th century was complemented by a significant change in the way houses were arranged that came about with the introduction of the fireplace. Before this time, most cottages in a village would have been open to the rafters with a hearth roughly in the centre of the main room and the smoke drifting up through the soot-covered thatched roof (see Fig 1.11). This arrangement lost favour when the gentry sought to divide up their houses to create more privacy and began trapping the smoke under hoods and later within fireplaces. They became something of a status symbol in the Tudor period, hence the often elaborately decorated tall chimneys. It was not until the following century that fireplaces became more common further down the social scale, and in East Anglia they only became a standard fitting in cottages from the late 1600s.

The introduction of fireplaces changed the way in which the cottage interior could be arranged. A fireplace meant that an upper floor could be

FIG 1.11: *A medieval longhouse with a byre for livestock at one end and a living area at the other, separated by a passage. This basic concept varied in size and layout depending upon the status of the occupant and local styles. The byre was divided into sections, although there may not have been any physical division at these points, just the line of the timber supports.*

inserted now that the space did not have to be open to vent the smoke, so a loft or bedroom area was created. As most cottages only had low walls at this date, this upper storey was lit by windows set in the gable ends or more usually by dormer windows built into the roof at the front. In single-roomed cottages, or older ones which were being upgraded, the chimney stack was built onto one end with just one fireplace in the ground floor room. In larger cottages, a popular arrangement was to build the brick stack between the two ground floor rooms with either a grate in the main living room or two back to back fireplaces. The front door usually opened next to the fireplaces, forming a small lobby, while stairs or a ladder to give access to the rooms above was fitted in the space at the rear. This lobby entrance plan was characteristic of cottages built in the late 17th and early 18th centuries.

Simple cottages like this continued to be built into the 19th century, by which time cheaper bricks and roof pantiles set at a lower pitch could cover a deeper house. This meant that double pile plans with rooms at the front and back were being built for the labouring classes. These early versions of the familiar urban terrace might only have a small second room at the rear but they were a big step up for the occupants with their full-height bedrooms and more windows which allowed better ventilation. However, space was still limited. There was usually only one fireplace downstairs and the building had to accommodate a whole family with boys and girls still using one bedroom.

Although cottage dwellers rarely had the income or security to make significant changes to these basic plans, they could make extensions when times were good. A low lean-to along the rear could provide room for a scullery, pantry or dairy without having to make major changes to the original walls or roof. Provision also had to be made for the cottage industries, fishing, and livestock. For these, outbuildings were

■ **Cottage orientation**

The position of a cottage on its plot of land is sometimes worthy of note. In the past, village buildings were usually arranged with their broad side facing the road or green, whereas in towns it was the narrow end which faced out. Hence the plots of land were broad and often of regular size, and although this is no longer the case it is sometimes possible to work out the original plan from old maps. However, some cottages were positioned with the short end facing the road. This was done for a variety of reasons. It often occurred down a hill, as the depth of excavation into the slope was less if the property ran along the contour. It might also indicate that the village was intended to be a small town with urban style plots, and it was common in the 19th century for a row of small terraced houses to be built in a line down an old single plot to get the most from rental returns.

FIG 1.12: *A common form of cottage or small house during the 17th and early 18th centuries had a large central fireplace and chimney stack, with the stairs and front door in line with them. This distinctive lobby entrance plan can still be recognised today in extended houses by the position of the chimney and original doorway.*

FIG 1.13: *Examples of cottages, with plans of their ground floors. The most basic cottage (left) had a single ground floor room, usually around 14-16 ft wide, and was common from the 17th to the 19th century. Some early examples did not have the fireplace. The larger two-roomed cottage (centre) with unheated bedrooms accessed by central stairs was common in the later 18th and early 19th century. In the Victorian period smaller terraces which were now two rooms deep (right) were built in either pairs or short rows.*

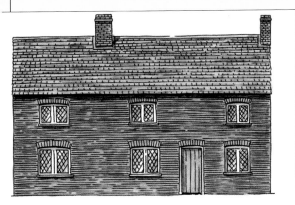

FIG 1.14: *Most labourers' homes in the 17th and early 18th century would have one ground floor room, the better examples with a second, although this might only be half as big as the first. Above this would have been one or two bedchambers, accessed by a ladder in the smallest cottages. The larger three-room plan shown here would have been intended for a superior tenant or a farmer with a small-holding.*

Parlour   Living room   Kitchen

usually added down one side of the plot rather than being attached to the cottage itself. Some had their walls heightened, and a new shallow-pitched roof installed (usually with pantiles replacing thatch) so making the loft a useable space.

As cottages became desirable homes in the 20th century so extensions were made to bring them up to modern standards. Extending in line or building a wing at one end was common. Some built up and back so a humble single-storey cottage was transformed into a more ordinary house. Although it may not be obvious at a glance, the original one or two-room core of the house built up against the old fireplace can usually still be traced.

FIG 1.15: *The side of a cottage can often reveal evidence of various stages of its construction and development.*

CHAPTER 2

Cottage Materials
Flint, mud and thatch

FIG 2.1: *East Anglian cottages are notable for the wide range of materials used, as in this example from Suffolk with brick, timber, thatch and tiles.*

GEOLOGY

Unlike regions of England where there is a principal building material which characterises the area, East Anglia lacks such a resource. There are no extensive outcrops of good building stone and many of the alternative materials were limited to isolated pockets. So although flint, timber and clay can be found across most areas, no single material is dominant. The result is the wide variety of textures and colours which are characteristic of Norfolk and Suffolk cottages.

Chalk underlies most of East Anglia, rising to the surface as a low ridge running north from Cambridge up to the east of King's Lynn. The harder parts of this outcrop, known as clunch, are sometimes used for building. On its western edge there is a thin line of crumbly sandstone, locally known as carstone, and beyond this are the clays and mud of the Fens. In the other direction the gently rolling landscape of the heart of East Anglia is made up of a softer chalk full of the flint which is widely used to form cottage walls. Above this are Ice-Age deposits of gravel, sand and clay, the last of which was used from an early date for mud walling, and later for the production of bricks and roof tiles. There are also local outcrops of stone-like crag and conglomerates (glacial deposits moulded together) which are occasionally used. Erosion by the sea and rivers has turned many of these stones into rounded pebbles which are a distinctive feature of many buildings in coastal districts especially in north Norfolk.

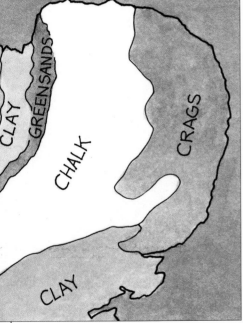

FIG 2.2: *A simplified map of the underlying geology of East Anglia. Over the top of this were layers of later sediments and glacial deposits which themselves provided some materials where the rock or clay below was not easy to obtain. Shallow pits in fields and small quarries around villages still survive today to remind us that most of the materials used in cottages were provided from the local landscape.*

MATERIALS
Flint
One of the materials commonly seen in East Anglian cottages is flint, a hard silica which occurs in chalk as nodules. It is believed that they are the remains of ancient sponges that lived in the shallow seas where the chalk formed, the slightly porous outer surface of each one absorbing some of the surrounding materials and forming a pale crust around each stone. It is most easily extracted in ploughed fields, in glacial deposits or by the coast where the sea has eroded the softer rock. Although it usually has a glossy black finish, there are subtle tones of blue, grey and brown which vary between the regions. Despite its rough shape and being hard to work, the durability and abundance of flint made it a popular building material. It was used in castles, churches and other important medieval buildings, the finest of which have flint worked into a glossy black square

FIG 2.3: *It is the variety of materials which builders had to resort to using in East Anglia which has created a kaleidoscope of cottages full of colour and texture. Top row, from left to right: brick, clunch (hard chalk), carstone, and pebbles. Bottom row: timber-frame, thatch and flint. Further variety is created with lime wash, tar or paint, as in the example on the bottom right.*

which creates a fine, smooth surface known as flushwork.

Flint was used in the construction of cottages from the 17th century. In these more humble buildings the walls were built either with the facing stones set randomly or in horizontal courses within a bed of lime mortar. Sometimes the mortar was so thick that very little of the flint was visible until the mortar

FIG 2.4: *Examples of flint showing how the colour can vary from browns to greys and blues. Most cottages had the stones randomly set within the walls with their white or brown outer surface exposed (left). However, in some examples they were carefully chosen and set in rough courses (centre). The most expensive finish used knapped and coursed flints (right) but these are only found in the finest houses or as a facing material in late-Victorian buildings.*

FIG 2.5: *Galleting is a distinctive finish found in many cottages in East Anglia. Small stones or shards of flint are inserted into wet mortar.*

started to weather away. In finer work the mortar was finished so it left the facing stones neatly framed (there is often less than 50 per cent flint in these walls where so much mortar and brick was used). A distinctive style has small shards of stone, known as gallets, inserted between the flints to create a speckled appearance in the mortar. These types of walls needed an occasional horizontal line of brick or masonry to act as a levelling course and to help lace the wall together. Flint was also unsuitable to form neat, durable corners so again brick or masonry was used (usually the former in the case of East Anglian cottages). The finished walls usually had a minimum width of around 18 inches, much thicker than a conventional brick wall.

Brick quoins   Rubble core

Facing stones

Brick lacing course

FIG 2.6: *Flint walls might appear to be a jumble of stones but there is more to them than meets the eye. Stones have to be carefully selected and positioned with an outer skin often set in rows and connected to a rubble core. When they are being built it is essential that some parts of the rough flints touch the surrounding ones so that as much weight from above is passed down through them, rather than through the mortar. Lime mortar was used as it is permeable and allows for some settlement and movement. Modern cement does not permit moisture to escape and is prone to cracking around the flints or through the wall. Today, flint is used only as a facing material set within a brick frame, the actual part which carries the load from the upper floors and roof is the block work inner leaf to which the facing material is tied.*

Pebbles

Along the coast or in river beds the weathering action of water turns stones into rounded pebbles. These were used in wall construction in a similar way to flint and examples can be found along the coast especially in north Norfolk. Pebbles were popular especially in the second half of the 19th century and are often found as a facing material set within the facade of Victorian terraces as well as in cottages. In some regions these were tarred or colour-washed to protect the wall from the effects of the coastal weather.

FIG 2.7: *Pebbles in walls could either be randomly set, as in the cottages on the left, or they could be arranged in courses, as on the right. The Victorians loved this effect and used pebbles on many of their houses in the north of Norfolk, where they tend to be very regular and tightly packed with little mortar showing.*

Masonry

While the wealthy could bring in limestone or sandstone from other regions the ordinary cottage builder usually had to use something closer to hand. One of these local resources was the brown and ochre sandstone known as carstone which can be seen in cottages in the Downham Market and Hunstanton area of north-west Norfolk. The small size of workable pieces meant that it was often used in a similar way to flint, with brick used for corners and levelling courses. It could be squared off into small blocks in the

finest work though it was more commonly used as rough pieces set randomly, or set in courses with gallets in the mortar. In the late 19th century it became fashionable to use flat slabs of carstone (slips or tiles) which were laid on each other with the mortar so deeply recessed that it was barely visible.

Clunch is a particularly hard layer of chalk which can be used as a building material. It could be picked up from ploughed land but was usually quarried. Clunch contains a lot of water when in the ground so is easy to cut into blocks, and then it hardens as it dries. It can sometimes be found in cottage walls, mixed with other stones or bricks, but was more commonly

FIG 2.8: *Examples of carstone from the area to the north-east of King's Lynn. Thin pieces were used on country estates such as Sandringham during the late 19th century (top).*

FIG 2.9: *Clunch walls could either be built with rough pieces randomly set in thick mortar, or cut down into blocks to make courses, as in this example.*

■ Foundations

Although we may assume that a cottage which has stood for centuries is more substantially built than a modern house, there are key areas where they lag behind. The value of good foundations was appreciated by some, but they were not always put into use until legislation in the late 19th century meant that a deep and sound base had to be created. Most flint, brick and stone cottages built before this time may have little more than the top soil removed, creating a shallow ditch in which the wall was built. Timber-framed and mud walls were built on a low stone or brick plinth which was usually set in a shallow ditch. As a result it is common to see old buildings which appear to sag or lean because they have settled onto their poor foundations. If there are no fresh signs of movement then this should not be of concern. The nature of the materials in old buildings, and the use of lime mortar, means that they have a degree of flexibility and can tolerate slight movement and fluctuations in moisture levels more than modern buildings. However, there can be changes to the local environment like a rising water table, the growth of trees and shrubs, paved or tarmac drives, increased road traffic and cracked drains, all of which can cause the ground to rise and fall. East Anglia is also particularly prone to shrinkable clay soils which contain high levels of water and often cause problems. Any fresh signs of movement in the walls should be investigated.

FIG 2.10: *Some cottage walls were poorly constructed or had later changes which caused them to buckle, bow or crack. Flint, pebble and stone walls which were not correctly laid so the facing stones bonded to the rubble core, or were not well tied to the inner leaf in more modern construction, can bow and even fall away from the house. It is quite common to see these supported either by a buttress or by iron or steel rods which run under the floorboards from one side to the other. Discs or straps are exposed on the outside, as in these examples.*

FIG 2.11: *Due to limited building resources in East Anglia it is common to find a mixture of materials in cottage walls. Sometimes broken pieces of brick were mixed into the rubble core of a flint wall, but they could also be seen on the exterior surface. The examples here, on the left and centre, show flint, clunch and a variety of coloured bricks exposed on the face of the wall. It is likely that the builder never expected these to be seen and they would have probably been whitewashed or rendered. In some cases, however, it was used for decorative effect, especially in the Victorian period. The materials were carefully arranged to create a pattern, as in the example on the right, with carstone, pebbles and brick.*

used in garden walls or farm buildings where its susceptibility to erosion was less of a concern. There are other isolated pockets of stones which have been used for building, such as septaria, a brown ironstone found along the coast near Orford which has been used in a limited number of houses in a restricted area, adding to the architectural variety of the region.

Brick

Probably the most common material found in East Anglian cottages is brick. It was used not just for the main walls but in the corners, chimneys and floors of houses built from other materials.

With little good building stone, plenty of suitable clay and a proximity to the Low Countries where brick-making skills were well established in the medieval period, it was along the east coast where the first brick buildings were erected, probably during the 13th century. Over the following three to four hundred years it was used for only the finest houses, appearing in more humble walls in conjunction with other materials, until it worked its way down the social ladder and was used in this region for the better cottages of the Georgian and Victorian periods. Before large scale brickworks began transporting their products all over the

FIG 2.12: *The colour of bricks varies depending upon the clay used, the length of firing time and the position of the bricks in the kiln. Rich red was the most common colour across East Anglia but a light beige (often referred to as white) can be found around Ipswich and Cambridge, and in parts of west Norfolk. Burnt bricks with a grey finish were often used to create decorative effects especially in the 16th century and then again in the early 19th century. The oldest bricks tend to vary in size and have a rough finish. Examples from the 18th and early 19th century are more regular and set in a distinct bond, while later mass-produced bricks usually have a consistent colouring and sharper edges. A useful aid in the dating of bricks is the presence of a frog – the recess in the top and bottom which was introduced in the early 19th century. Flat bricks will usually date from before this. In the example here, the finer white bricks on the left have been used for the facade while the older red bricks are down the side of the building.*

country in the second half of the 19th century, the bricks used in this region reflected the colour and texture of the local clay and firing method. Initially this process was performed close by the houses for which they were used. The clay was extracted, dried and fired in a kiln for a single building project. Permanent kilns and brickworks were established during the 17th century as the use of brick became more widespread.

A solid brick wall has stretchers (a brick laid lengthways) on the inner and outer side, between which the headers (with the short end exposed) are placed at intervals to hold the two sides together. The arrangement of headers and stretchers is referred to as the bond or bonding. Flemish bond, with alternate headers and stretchers on each course, was dominant in the 18th and 19th centuries. English bond, which had a course of headers followed by one of stretchers was widely used in the 16th and 17th centuries and was revived in the late 19th century. These required a large number of bricks so it was common for a few courses of stretchers to be laid and then a single row of headers, to save on cost.

The standard of brickwork in poorer cottages may not have been up to that of finer houses. Speculative builders were notorious for taking short cuts and many late 18th and early 19th-century houses can still suffer from poor workmanship. Problems often arose when the builder broke bricks in half and used each end as a header, this saved money but meant the wall was not correctly bonded. It was also

FIG 2.13: *Examples of English bond (top), Flemish bond (centre) and rat trap bond (bottom). Ordinary bricklaying is shown to the left in the lower picture to give some idea of the larger size of the courses in rat trap bond.*

■ **Mortar**

Mortar is used between bricks and stones to spread the load from the floors and roof and to seal the wall against the elements. Lime was an essential ingredient as it helped the mortar stick to the bricks and stones, allowed moisture to escape, and made the wall more tolerant of movement. From the late 19th century, cement-based mortars were widely used. These are generally impervious to water and are stronger, complementing the properties of modern bricks. However, the use of cement-based mortars to repair older porous brickwork can often cause problems. Cracks appear that allow water into the wall. If the trapped moisture freezes, the face of the brick can flake away and eventually disintegrate.

common for pieces of timber to be inserted in walls to correct a level, or for fixings to be attached to. These can slowly rot away causing the brickwork to crack. With the introduction of a brick tax in 1784 (to help pay for the American War of Independence) by which the builder was charged for every 1000 bricks used, ways were devised to reduce the number, including the production of larger bricks. Another method which reduced the number of bricks was the rat trap bond in which bricks were laid on their side so they are taller on the outer face. This unfortunately lacked the stability of other bonds and created a void which filled with rain water and caused damp.

Timber framing

A large framework of timber with the gaps filled to complete the walls was the standard method of construction for the better class of late-medieval house. However, in East Anglia during this period, suitable local wood was becoming scarce, especially in Norfolk, and as a result timber-framed houses are more commonly found in Suffolk. Most timber-framed cottages were originally of high status but later fell down the social scale as owners moved to larger, more fashionable homes. Some are part of old farm and manor houses which were split up to form labourers' homes at a later date. Purpose-built cottages made from timber framing in the 17th century exist but these tend to be of a more flimsy appearance with wider gaps between thinner timbers reflecting the difficulty in sourcing suitable local wood. By this time timber-framing had

FIG 2.14: *Closely fitted vertical posts (top left) were distinctive of East Anglia in the 15th and 16th centuries and were something of a status symbol. As good timber became scarce, thinner pieces spaced further apart were used (top right and bottom). These tend to date from the 17th or 18th centuries. Originally wattle and daub was fitted between the posts, and the panels were lime or colour washed (bottom), but from the 17th century this was often replaced by bricks in a herringbone pattern (top).*

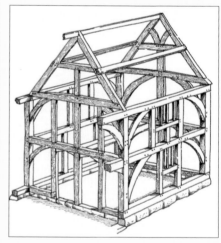

FIG 2.15: *One end of a medieval box frame house with the infill removed to show the basic structure. With the shortage of good timber in the 17th century, it was common for wood from old houses to be reused for a new building.*

fallen from favour and fine brickwork and masonry were fashionable. Numerous fires had resulted in timber-framed buildings being banned from many urban areas.

Oak was the timber of choice although other woods were often used for certain parts of the building, like pine which was imported in bulk through Norfolk's ports as early as the 15th century. The frame was made up from a carefully engineered structure of vertical posts and horizontal beams which supported the roof and upper floors (box framing). Early work tends

to have large square panels with thick timber and strong bracing pieces. In the late 15th and 16th centuries close studding with tightly spaced verticals was a fashionable display of wealth and ambition. The gaps between were originally filled with wattle and daub, a wicker work of sticks coated with a rough rendering inside and out, although these were often later replaced by brick or mud blocks. The exterior would have originally been white or colour washed to protect the walls, it is not always clear if the timbers were left exposed to fade to their natural silvery grey (black coated timbers were a Victorian fashion). By the 17th century it became common to render over the timbers which aided fire resistance and covered up the

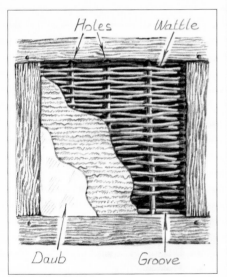

FIG 2.16: *A sketch showing how wattle and daub was created between the timbers. A frame of sticks (the wattle) was covered with layers of clay, straw and other local materials (the daub). The holes and grooves where the wattle was fitted into the timbers can sometimes be found where the original wattle and daub has been removed.*

FIG 2.17: *In East Anglia it was common to see timber-framed houses with brick gable ends, as here at the Old Vicarage, Methwold. These were either part of the original build or were added at a later date.*

wooden frame as they become un-fashionable. Pargetting was popular around this time, especially in Suffolk, although most examples found today are modern reproductions (see p 50).

Clay or mud walls

Clay or mud was once the most common building material for the walls of the poorest houses in a village. It

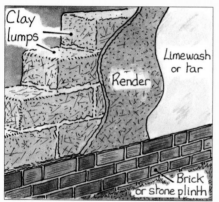

FIG 2.18: *A sketch showing how clay lump walls could be built up and coated. These materials allow the walls to breath and help remove any moisture from within. Modern cement renders and similar non-breathable coverings can cause serious damage to earth-built houses and should be replaced. It is also important to keep water away from a clay lump wall, so make sure guttering is not blocked and that garden levels have not built up around it so they cover the plinth. Any render coating should finish short of the ground so the plinth is exposed. Injected damp-proof courses and concrete floors can also cause problems as they prevent water moving as intended.*

■ Condensation

Condensation can cause black mould in houses and more serious damage to clay lump walls. It is caused when air with a high moisture content hits a cold surface like a window or an un-insulated wall and turns back into water droplets. Air entering houses through draughty windows and doors helps with ventilation but now, with the drive for energy efficiency, these are being sealed up. To reduce the problem try and ventilate the house as often as possible, avoid using tumble dryers or put them in an outhouse or garage, insulate the inner surface of exterior walls or use a dehumidifier.

could be used in a number of ways. Mud and stud was a popular method for constructing agricultural workers' homes, especially in the Fens up to the 19th century. A flimsy timber frame was assembled using thin bits of wood, with split lengths nailed over this. Then a mix of clay, straw and lime was applied to the framework with a large fork. When this had dried it was coated with whitewash to protect it. These flimsy homes had a short life and are rare today.

More substantial buildings were made from clay lumps. These were widely used for single-storey cottages from the late 18th to the early 20th century. Local clay was mixed with straw, chalk and gravel and was puddled by a horse or cow in a pit to make it pliable. It was then formed into rectangular blocks of approximately 18 x 9 x 6 inches and left to harden. These large unfired bricks were used to build a thick wall on top of a short stone or brick plinth (which kept the base away from damp) with clay slip or lime mortar used as a cement. The completed wall could be finished in a number of ways. A clay coating followed by one of tar and sand with a final coat of limewash was used in the 19th century.

Clay lump houses are mainly found in central East Anglia and can date from as late as the early 20th century when George Skipper used the material to build a series of council houses in the villages of East Harling and Garboldisham. With their protective coating, mud houses can look similar to rendered timber-frame houses and it can be hard to tell them apart at a glance.

ROOFING MATERIALS
Thatch

Thatch is one of the most ancient methods of roofing. Using readily available local materials such as straw, reed, heather, turf, and sedge, it was accessible to all and easy to maintain. Thatch was widely used in the medieval period but fell from favour in many towns, as closely packed thatched roofs enable fire to spread rapidly. By the late 17th century it was rare in urban areas. In the country its use continued into the Victorian period and the number of thatched houses actually grew in the first half of the 19th century in East Anglia as agriculture boomed.

FIG 2.19: *Examples of thatch from East Anglia with gable ends and the roof overhanging (bottom) or where the thatch is protected by an extended wall (top left). In order for the thatch to throw rain off the building rather than soak through its layers, the roof has to be at a steeper pitch than most other roofs, usually around 50 to 55°. Today the ridge is often raised into a block form with a shaped profile but in the past it was more usual for it to be flush with the main surface of the roof. Note how the eaves are cut so that water is thrown clear of the walls below. The habit of standing on the area of ground where the rain lands – the eavesdrop – means you might hear some gossip through an open window.*

However by this time it was associated with poverty, covering as it did, the homes of the poor. As mass-produced pantiles, slates and corrugated iron became available, so thatch was replaced rather than renewed. With the popularity of combine harvesters after the Second World War the supply of suitable straw for roofing dried up with the effect that of the one million thatched roofs that existed in 1800 only about 35,000 survived in 1960. Today there are approximately 24,000 listed houses with thatched roofs, the majority being in a strip across England from Devon and Dorset, through the Home Counties, and on into Suffolk and Essex.

Just as the use of thatch declined, so

it began to be appreciated as something rustic, traditional and rural. Arts and Crafts architects at the turn of the 20th century sought to revive traditional methods and a number of their houses included thatched roofs. Today they have become something of a desirable luxury for the cottage owner and thatch is being reinstated, or included in new houses. The use of renewable materials with such good insulation properties creates more potential for future use.

There are three types of thatched roofs in England. Reed was limited to the Norfolk Broads and a few coastal areas where it grew in sufficient quantities. Much of what is used today is imported. The finished surface is

FIG 2.20: *A drawing of a roof being thatched. The straw or reeds are laid from the eaves upwards with the bundles spread out over the battens and temporarily held by reeding pins (1). The surface is then dressed with a legget, a wooden bat with a ridged surface, to form an even surface (2). This is fixed by sways - metal rods in this example - held down by stainless steel wire fixed to screws driven into the rafters (3). Traditionally this was done with hazel spars or rope. The next course overhangs the previous, covering the sways until the top is reached. A ridge piece is formed to complete the roof. Lengths of hazel or willow called liggers, are used to hold down long straw around the eaves and verges of the completed roof, usually in the form of two lines with cross pieces between (see FIG 2.19). Wire netting is applied over straw to hold it in place in exposed locations and keep birds and vermin away. Reed does not usually require this.*

■ Fire

A major problem with a thatched roof is its vulnerability to catching fire. In many cases when a thatched cottage has burnt down it is found that the cause was a wood-burning stove, either because sparks were created by an unsuitable fuel or the intense heat caused combustion in the chimney. The risk can be reduced by using only seasoned or kiln-dried wood in a burner and ensuring that the flue has a suitable liner. Also make sure the chimney is well maintained and that it stands at least 6ft above the ridge with a pot no greater than 2ft high. Any electrics in the cottage should be regularly checked as faulty wiring is another common cause of fire. Also ensure any contractor working on or around the roof has sufficient public liability insurance as the risk of fire is often greater when building or maintenance work is being carried out. You can also have fire retardant boards fitted under the thatch to protect the rest of the house if the roof catches fire (these need to be fitted with a suitable gap so moisture does not get trapped in the thatch). There are new sprays which are designed to reduce flammability but their long-term effect on the thatch is not yet known.

smooth with the butt ends flush and a raised or block ridge formed out of straw as it is more flexible than reed.

Combed wheat reed is straw which has been specially prepared for thatching and creates a finish similar to that of reed but the completed roof tends to be more rounded in appearance. The long straw method uses straw which is not so neatly aligned but is laid out and wetted before being applied. This makes it more pliable and creates a more ragged finish with both ears and butt ends visible on the surface. These are then gathered into yealms - the bundles which are carried onto the roof to be laid. This method is usually distinguished by the lines of liggers (thin wooden rods which form lines to hold down the thatch) around the eaves and verges, not just the ridge as in the other methods. Despite reed being a distinctive feature of the Broads it is likely that straw was more widely used over much of East Anglia in the past.

A good thatch roof can last up to 50 years without maintenance, although the ridge tends to require work every 10-15 years. Reed is more durable than straw but the longevity of thatch is determined more by the quality of the work, the local climate and how exposed each face is to the elements. When the surface material has rotted down or been blow away, so that the sways and spars which hold each course down are becoming exposed, then it is time for replacement. A reed roof is regarded as a one-coat covering to be completely replaced when its time is up, however straw can have just its upper layer (coatwork) renewed leaving the old base in place. There are some examples of medieval thatch still in existence where this method of renewal has been repeated over the centuries, with their underside blackened by smoke from open fires that burned over five hundred years ago.

Plain clay tiles

The main alternatives to thatch were plain clay roofing tiles which became available alongside the bricks used in the 13th century. These were made from clay which was rolled or cut out into thin rectangles of roughly 10 x 6 inches, typically with two holes close to one edge for fixing. When they were fired they tended to curl slightly, and they varied in colour and texture according to the local clay and their position in the kiln. The roof had horizontal battens nailed across the rafters and the tiles were fixed by wooden pegs so they hung over them. Plain clay tiles were double lapped so that only around four inches of the tile was exposed. They are more

FIG 2.21: *Traditional plain clay tiles (top) and pantiles (bottom). A tile has been omitted in the centre of each photo to show how clay tiles have more of an overlap than pantiles.*

often found on houses which have later become cottages rather than being used on original labourers' homes, and are commonly found in western and central Suffolk but rarely in the coastal region.

Pantiles

Around the coast of East Anglia and across much of Norfolk a distinctive type of clay tile was used called pantiles (the word 'pan' is confusingly Dutch for 'tile'). These have a distinctive shallow 's' profile with an edge which interlocks across the top of a neighbouring tile. They are also larger, being roughly 13 x 9 inches, and as a result are more widely spaced. They overlap only a small part

FIG 2.22: *A close up of the eaves of a pantile roof showing how a tile hooks over its neighbour. Pantiles were not normally nailed in place but had a nib which hung off the battens making them vulnerable to the wind along the exposed edges of the roof. Where this happened the gable wall could be extended upwards by a few courses to protect it. This solution was also used to protect thatch roofs so although a roof may now be covered in pantiles it could have originally been thatched. There may also be a line of protruding bricks around the chimney which helped keep rainwater away from the junction with the thatch.*

FIG 2.23: *Examples of red and black pantiles. Black glazed pantiles were often used for sections of the roof which were visible from the road, with cheaper unglazed ones on other parts. From the late Victorian period a wider range of profiled tiles became available which can sometimes be found on cottages.*

of the tile below which makes them lighter and able to be set at a lower pitch than plain clay tiles. Pantiles first appeared as imports from the Low Countries, hence their frequent use along the east coast. They were widely used on houses in this region in the 17th century with locally produced versions becoming widespread in the following century. Their relative low cost and light weight made them an ideal replacement for thatch on many houses and they were the standard roofing material for most cottages until the late 19th century. Most were unglazed and orange/red in colour but glazed versions became available from the mid 18th century which were less prone to frost damage. A distinctive black type was popular in parts of East Anglia.

■ Looking after tiled roofs

The durability of a tiled roof depends on a number of factors, including the quality of the tile itself. The pitch needs to be at the correct angle so that water runs off effectively - around 40° for plain clay tiles and as low as 25° for pantiles. The amount of rainfall and sunlight each face experiences will have an effect, as will exposure to strong winds which can dislodge tiles. Damage can also be caused by climbing plants like ivy, and moving tree branches, while every roof is vulnerable to damage caused by people walking across it. In time the roof will inevitably start to deteriorate as tiles, battens, pegs and nails rot or fail.

It is important with a period property regularly to check the roof for faults like a dislodged or cracked tile and for problems with the ridge and flashing around chimneys. Also make sure that the verges are sound, guttering and valleys are clear and any downpipes are not loose or cracked. If work is necessary then check that contractors are familiar with the traditional methods and materials. Cementing under tiles and the use of certain waterproof membranes may not be suitable. They should also try to retain as many of the original tiles as possible. For a complete replacement of the roof, scaffolding would be required, therefore it would also be a good time to check the chimney and gable walls, and have any features like new aerials fitted.

CHAPTER 3

Cottage Details
Windows, doors and other features

FIG 3.1: *Although building materials give a cottage its regional distinction, it is the details like windows, doors and porches which create the character, as in this row at Castle Rising, Norfolk.*

Cottages gain their romanticised image not only from their rustic walls and deep overhanging thatched roofs but also from their fixtures and fittings. Small hinged windows, planked doors and rickety chimneys were essential components of late Victorian paintings of rural houses and these neatly proportioned and simple features remain important for an authentic look. They were never originally chosen for aesthetic reasons – windows and doors were small because ceilings were low and budgets were tight. Before mass-produced items flooded the market in the late 19th century these fittings were made from local materials by artisans working in the area, their style reflecting contemporary tastes but with some unique detail exclusive to a craftsman, region or estate.

The size and quality of these details can give clues about the origins of a building. A cottage with large window openings, grand doorways and carved decoration would once have been a house of higher status, those whose original details are small and plain are more likely to have been of humble origin. The style and materials used for the details can also help date a structure

FIG 3.2: *A medieval mullion window which was originally unglazed, with horizontally sliding wooden shutters on the inside to keep out the elements.*

although care should be taken. Some 18th and 19th-century cottages might have retained some original features but most would have been replaced, especially during renovations in the past century. The following sections outline some styles of fittings used through the ages which can help in understanding a building or help those restoring a cottage to find appropriate parts.

Windows

Windows were originally created as much for ventilation as to allow light in, the word comes from the old Norse term for 'wind-eye', and most domestic types from the medieval period were open to the elements. To keep out unwanted draughts, hinged or sliding wooden shutters were fitted and there are records showing that oiled linen, wooden lattices and flattened pieces of animal horn were also used. Glass was reserved for only the finest buildings before the 16th century. The frames of these early windows were part of the timber frame of the building with the opening divided by vertical posts called mullions. Larger windows had a horizontal piece called a transom between rows of mullions. In the finest examples arch-shaped pieces of carved timber were inserted at the top of each opening for decorative effect.

Glazed windows with small pieces of glass held by lead strips became common in urban areas during the Tudor period but were not widely adopted in rural cottages until the late 17th century (FIG 3.4). Such was their value before this date that glazed

Stanchion.

Lead cames.

Turnbuckle catch.

Wrought iron Frame.

Handle

Stay

FIG 3.3: *The squared vertical mullions were positioned so that the sharp edge faced out. When these are removed a distinctive diamond-shaped hole is left in the head beam and sill. These can often be found when old windows are restored. Old mullion windows are often found blocked up (top) or have been adapted for more modern glazing (bottom). They can also be seen tucked down the side or rear of a building where the old fashioned style is out of sight and has never been updated.*

FIG 3.4: *A hinged light in a glazed 17th-century casement window with diamond-shaped pieces of glass (quarrels) set within a mesh of lead strips (cames). This would have been hung on metal pintles on the outside. It would have a catch to lock the window shut, a handle for opening it and a stay to hold it open. Originally these fittings would have been produced by a local blacksmith and could have details which were unique to a local area. As most surviving windows probably date from the last 200 years their fittings are more likely to be mass-produced versions with a simple design. However the Arts and Crafts Movement of the late 19th and early 20th centuries delighted in creating decorative ironwork and many cottages built under their influence could have beautifully detailed pieces. Fittings were nearly always made of iron. Brass was only affordable after the Napoleonic wars and was rarely used in rural cottages.*

windows would have been taken by the occupant when they moved house.

By the 18th century, wooden casement windows had become common in cottages across the region.

FIG 3.5: *Examples of casement windows. 17th-century types (top left) would have diamond-shaped glass pieces. By the second half of the 18th century, timber glazing bars and segmental headed windows were becoming common (top centre). In the Victorian period larger pieces of glass were available (top right and bottom left) while Arts and Crafts architects loved long, low windows (bottom right).*

These were simple square or rectangular frames typically with two or three lights divided by a few horizontal glazing bars. This style continued to be used throughout the 19th century, often with a shallow segmental brick arch above, to bear the load from above. By this time iron-framed windows were also available, some of which were cast into elaborate patterns imitating earlier Tudor or Elizabethan types. These are often found on cottages belonging to a country estate where a whole batch could have been made in a distinctive style. In the late Victorian period timber mullion windows with leaded glass were revived as 16th and 17th-century houses inspired Arts and Crafts architects.

FIG 3.6: *Iron and timber casement windows with elaborate patterns were distinctive of many country estate cottages especially during the early and mid 19th century.*

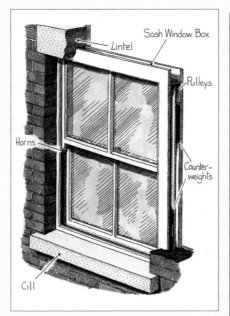

FIG 3.7: *A cut away showing the workings of a vertically hung sash window. Horns were added from around the 1840s to strengthen the joints.*

FIG 3.8: *An 18th-century sash window (top left), a 19th-century one with larger panes of glass (top right) and a Yorkshire sash (bottom).*

■ Window maintenance

Local conservation and listed building regulations may limit an owner's ability to replace old draughty windows with modern double-glazed units but there are now ways of upgrading existing fittings which can meet energy efficiency demands without losing the valued appearance of the property. There are specialists who can repair original windows or supply authentic replacements for any not worth saving. Broken glass or rotten wood can be replaced and the layers of paint which can make windows hard to open can be removed. Thin brush strips can be inserted around openings to make them airtight, and fittings and pulleys can be repaired to make the renovated window secure and operate smoothly. To further improve energy efficiency and noise reduction, discreet secondary glazing can be added. It is also worth remembering that original windows have probably lasted at least a hundred years whereas many modern uPVC units may need replacing after only 20 years or so. Repairing original fittings will not only satisfy local authorities, but may also have a positive effect on the property's value and save money in the long term.

FIG 3.9: *Dormer windows were often the best way to get light into a cottage with low walls and bedrooms in the loft space.*

FIG 3.10: *Dormer windows can be found in a variety of forms. Some are extensions of the lower wall (bottom left) others are set within the roof (top right). The flat-capped style of this latter example is very characteristic of East Anglian cottages.*

FIG 3.11: *Segmental arches (top) are common on late 18th and 19th-century cottages. Square headed brickwork with diagonally set bricks and a keystone are distinctive of some Norfolk and Fenland cottages (bottom).*

Although vertical sash windows were common in most towns their height did not suit the low walls of rural cottages. Only in the Victorian terraces found in most East Anglian villages were they originally fitted. Some older cottages had them squeezed in later as an owner attempted to make a humble abode more fashionable. However, Yorkshire sash windows were widely used in cottages as an alternative to casement windows especially in the late 18th and early 19th centuries. As these moved sideways in grooves they did not need weights and pulleys and were thus cheaper to make.

Shutters

Shutters were an important part of unglazed medieval and Tudor windows and could have been fitted on the inside or outside, hinging up or down or sliding across. Although these do not survive today, the marks where they were fitted can sometimes be found in the timbers of an original window. External louvre or panelled shutters were fashionable in towns and cities of the 18th and early 19th centuries. Originals may not have survived but the metal pintles and shutter stays can sometimes be found on the window frames and walls.

Doors

Original cottage doors were simple and plain, usually formed from vertical planks held together by horizontal battens on the inner face. The earliest of these plank and batten doors in domestic properties date from the 16th century and have two or three wide planks of irregular width. Four planks were more common in the 18th century and six in the 19th century, by which time the planks were machine cut so were regular in size and sharp edged. In older doors the planks were usually butted up against each other, then from the 17th century they were rebated to cover any gaps that appeared as the wood dried. A vertical bead moulding edged planks in 18th and 19th century doors.

On the finer houses these simple doors might be decorated. The nails which pinned the planks to the battens were arranged in patterns enhanced with scratched marks between them, or vertical strips called fillets were applied over the butt joint which also helped hide any gaps. In the 17th century a wide variety of designs were created by these applied fillets or with the use of thinner carved strips between the wider planks, many of these imitating the panelling which was becoming fashionable inside the house during this period. These more elaborate plank and batten doors would never have been fitted in a labourer's home but if

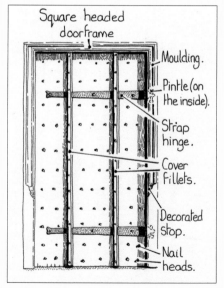

FIG 3.12: *A 16th-century plank and batten door with labels highlighting the details (most cottage doors would have been less decorative than this). As shortages of timber affected Norfolk and Suffolk, doors with narrower planks became common from the 17th century.*

FIG 3.13: *Examples of doors, from a 16th-century plank and batten style (far left) to 19th-century panelled types (far right). Note how the 19th and 20th century plank and batten front doors (centre right) have a frame. Like windows, most timber work would either have been left in its original state or it would be treated with a protective lime wash as used on the walls. Cottages associated with a country estate usually had their doors painted in the same colour. In the Victorian period there was more of a choice but most doors were either stained or grained so that they appeared to be a better quality hardwood, or they were painted a dark colour. It was not until the 20th century that the wide range of finishes and bright colours were applied to cottage doors.*

they are found today it could imply that the cottage was once of a higher status or that it has been removed from another house.

True panelled doors only became widely available in the 18th century. They would not have been fitted to labourers' cottages except perhaps those associated with a country estate, until cheaper mass-produced doors in the later Victorian period became standard even in village terraces. With the revival of traditional forms of building in the late 19th and early 20th century, plank and batten doors once again became fashionable.

Doors with glazed upper sections became popular from the late 19th century and have been fitted in many cottages recently to lighten up a room or hallway into which they open. In fact many cottage doors today are replica plank and batten types with a glass section, or panelled doors added at a later date. Originals have rarely survived because of their rudimentary appearance, poor condition or because they made the interior too dark.

The doors on most medieval and Tudor houses were designed to butt up against the rear of the frame and were not rebated within it, as on later examples. This means they would have been wider than the opening they were designed to cover. Rebated door frames only become common from the late

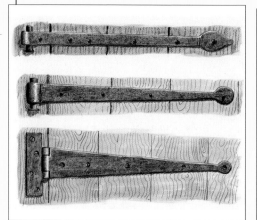

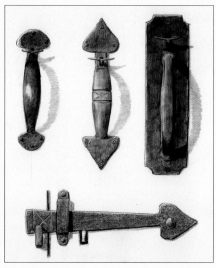

FIG 3.14: *Early strap hinges were made by the blacksmith. They tended to be long and thin, sometimes with an expanded or decorated end like the spearhead which was popular from the 16th to early 18th century (top). During the 17th century, hinges become slightly more pointed along their length. During the 18th century they were only used on cheaper houses and service rooms so they tended to be plain with a more pronounced taper (centre). In the Victorian period machine-made hinges with a metal plate to be screwed to the door frame were common (bottom).*

FIG 3.15: *Doors were held shut by simple iron latches on their inner face (bottom) although early ones could have been made from wood. Handles on the front would have been iron rings which turned to lift the latch, or a vertical handle with a thumb press, as in the 17th-century and Victorian examples (top left, centre and top right).*

17th century. The solid frame which surrounded the opening was usually square-headed in cottages but finer examples could have the door head carved into a shallow point or flat arch with moulding around the edge of the frame. The door was fixed to the frame by long iron strap hinges which ran across the front of the door. One end of the strap was bent round into a loop and hung over a metal pin called a pintle which was fixed into the door frame. From the 19th century machine-made types which incorporated a screw plate were used.

Porches

Labourers' cottages would not have the front door protected from the elements, however some estate cottages may have had a brick or timber porch added, to enhance the appearance of the cottage. Although rarely part of the original building, porches are a common later

FIG 3.16: *Porches would usually only be found on estate cottages (top) or as later additions to earlier buildings (bottom). Brick porches which are part of the original design will have their brick or stonework tied into the main walls whereas in later additions the brickworks will usually not line up and appear to be built up against it.*

addition to humble cottages. Tiled storm porches or timber-framed structures covered in climbing plants can add charm if not authenticity to an otherwise plain facade.

Gables

A notable feature of East Anglian cottages is the way roofs have a gable end rather than sloping down on all four sides (hipped roofs). Some have this wall extended above the roof line, which has the advantage of protecting the edge of the thatch or tiles from the wind, especially along the vulnerable coastal areas. A range of designs of gable end walls has been used over the centuries, many of which are a distinctive feature of East Anglia. Stepped gables were popular in the 16th century but can also be found on some late-18th and 19th-century houses. Close contact with the Low

Roof timbers

One of the first places you should investigate in an old building is the loft space. It can reveal so much about the origins of a house, as it was often left untouched when changes were made elsewhere. The roof timbers were arranged in different ways over the centuries and their origin and style can help date a house. In most cottages there would be rafters running up to the ridge and a purlin fixed horizontally along them. However, if you find a more elaborate arrangement, this could be a sign of an earlier or higher status building. Older roofs would have irregular pieces pegged together, later roofs or replacements used machine-cut timbers with nails and bolts.

Countries resulted in Dutch gables becoming popular. These feature concave and convex curves and right angles, and mostly date from the late 17th and early 18th century, although they were often revived during the 19th century. Characteristic of many gable ends in East Anglia are triangular sections of bricks along the top edge, set at 90° to the roof line and ending on a horizontal course of bricks. This is known as tumbled brickwork.

Wall finishes

Although many cottage walls are seen today as a pleasing mix of textures and colour, builders in the past would always have intended their work to appear to be something of finer quality. Rustic mixes of flints, bricks and mortar, or timber frames with thin, irregular members were often originally intended to be rendered, or were

FIG 3.17: *Examples of gables found on East Anglian buildings. In more exposed locations the end wall was extended upwards to protect the tiles from the wind (bottom). Where this is particularly high (as in the stepped gable centre right) it could mean the roof was once thatched. The gable ends of houses where the original material is exposed can often show how the building has changed. The example with the mansard roof (centre left) shows how the original flint wall has been extended with brickwork to make the new more spacious loft space.*

FIG 3.18: *An example of tumbled brickwork with triangles of diagonally arranged bricks lining the edge of the gable.*

FIG 3.20: *Bargeboards are fixed to the gable end of a roof to hide the ends of the roof timbers. Although they were usually plain on cottages, on some higher status timber-framed buildings they were carved into elaborate shapes especially in the 16th and early 17th century. They were also a favourite decorative feature of the Victorians who added ornamental pieces to their new and old houses alike. It is quite common to see a genuine 16th-century timber-framed house with elaborate 19th-century bargeboards. Mid-Victorian bargeboards had the most elaborate carvings but by the end of the century they were simpler, with just the underside shaped into a pattern.*

FIG 3.19: *Examples of Dutch gables which are so characteristic of the eastern seaboard.*

FIG 3.21: *Pargetting is the art of creating incised or raised patterns, symbols or figures in plaster or mortar on the exterior of a building. The word comes from the French 'parget' which itself was derived either from the word meaning to 'throw about' or 'to roughcast a wall' and originally applied to patterned render inside and outside. It is mainly associated with East Anglia, partly because it has survived here longer than in other areas. The principal parts used to make the render are lime, sand and animal hair, although other ingredients like cow dung, animal urine and road scrapings are also known to have been added. Designs range from simple geometric patterns stamped or incised into the wet render with nails in boards, combs and other tools, to more complex raised figures, symbols and heraldry which were moulded on the surface by skilled craftsmen. The finished work was lime or colour washed over. Some patterns are known to have been painted with colours although it is not clear if this was a common practice. The fashion for pargetting the exterior of houses seems to gather pace in the 16th century and reached a peak in the early to mid 17th century before falling out of fashion by the early 18th. Strapwork, which consisted of linked geometric shapes (above centre and right) was popular from the 1580s to the 1620s. It is hard to accurately date pargetting just from the style as it could have been repaired and remade several times, or could be a modern creation.*

covered up at a later date when they became unfashionable. It is only in the past century that tastes have changed and the original surface has been exposed.

A very distinctive feature of East Anglian cottages is pargetting. This is stamped, incised or moulded patterns on exterior plasterwork. Although it was popular in the 17th century it is likely that most of the pargetting we see today dates from the past hundred years, or has been repaired and adapted a number of times.

FIG 3.22: *Chimneys are always worth making note of when investigating cottages. Buildings may have been extended, clad, or rebuilt over the years, but the chimney is usually left as it was. A central rectangular brick base with circular or hexagonal stacks (bottom right) are signs that a cottage was of high status in the 16th or 17th centuries. These were copied during the 19th century (top right) usually with more decorative shafts and caps. Many cottages had brick stacks added at a later date so were built up on the outside and the full height of the stack is exposed (top left). Later examples were usually part of the original build and would have been plain and simple (bottom left).*

■ **The Dutch influence**

Much is made of the connection between East Anglia and the Low Countries and how it has influenced the style of houses built here. There is no doubt that these close trading partners shared many skills and techniques. Brick making, which had ended after the Roman period, was reintroduced from the 13th century via this avenue and pantiles were imported from the Low Countries before domestic production took over. There was also a large Dutch population in the eastern counties during the 17th century, perhaps making 30 per cent of the population at one time. No surprise then, that Dutch gables were popular. However, East Anglian cottages do, on the whole, follow the style of neighbouring counties rather than neighbouring countries.

FIG 3.23: *The name of a cottage can often be a clue to its past use, as in this example from Suffolk. Sometimes the name of a neighbouring property or field can also highlight a trade or industry which a cottage may have been associated with.*

51

FIG 3.24: *Although East Anglian cottages are found in many different colours there is little evidence that they were all finished this way originally. Paintings and literature show most rural timber-framed and mud houses with a protective coat of lime wash which resulted in a white or off-white coating (right) while brick houses were left in their natural finish. Some colour was used to pick out details, mullions were sometimes painted dark grey in the 17th century, window and door frames were often green with white walls, or off-white against red brick walls during the 18th century. It was not until the 19th century that colour seems to have been widely added to the exterior of rural cottages. Pink is most closely associated with Suffolk (top left). The colour was originally created with bulls' blood but later red ochre was used. Yellow ochre was also common (bottom left). Black or dark brown painted timber was a Victorian fashion which made use of industrial by-products such as coal tar. If choosing a suitable colour for a house today (where listed building consent does not restrict your choice) white, off-white, or an earthy tone made from local natural pigments would be authentic. Local authorities will be able to give advice.*

CHAPTER 4

▨ *The Cottage Interior* ▨
Don't forget to duck!

FIG 4.1: *This 19th-century cottage interior has a certain charm but closer inspection reveals the cracked walls, cramped space, and limited furnishings. Many villagers had to endure poverty and hardship through their whole lives.*

If a 19th-century labourer could see his cottage today he would probably recognise it from the outside, even though he might wonder why the owners had stripped off the render to expose a rickety timber frame. However if he stepped inside he would think he had walked into a palace. Our ideas of a charming rustic cottage with furniture, wood burner, carpets and the latest in luxury goods would be in stark contrast to the dark, dank and largely bare home he would have known 200 years earlier.

It is likely that most labourers were living in homes which, apart from a few new additions like a fireplace, had changed little since the Tudor period. Inventories from wills reveal that most had little more than a room or two, with just the bare essentials of somewhere to cook, sit and sleep and any additional items usually related to their line of work. Only a few people in a village would have acquired finer trimmings like plate racks with their best crockery on display, larger pieces of furniture such as dressers, or fabric curtains and a colourful rug. Most occupants of a cottage worked very long hours and were tenants who probably felt that they might be evicted at any time. They received such low pay that there was nothing left over for the finer things in life.

The earliest cottages would have the main living space centred on an open

FIG 4.2: *A medieval cottage interior at the Weald & Downland Open Air Museum in West Sussex. It shows how the room was open to the roof with a hearth in the centre and the most basic of fittings. Note the wooden shutter covering the small window in the back wall and the compacted earth floor.*

A Victorian labourer

The 19th-century cottage dweller in this region, deprived of land by the enclosures, was most likely to be a labourer working the land. They would work on the harvest, do hedge-laying or look after livestock, or they could be a boatman or a fisherman. While some cottage tenants worked on the land, others in the family might be in service working for the landowner. Most labouring families needed another source of income so some worked at home, spinning, weaving or carrying out other crafts. It may seem hard to believe that such large families all fitted into such a limited space, but it should be remembered that the family would rarely all be in the cottage together. Many adults went straight to the local hostelry after working all day, many of the daily chores could be done in the garden and children would play outside if they were not already put out to work in the fields.

FIG 4.3: *This interior from a black house on the Isle of Lewis demonstrates the smokey, cramped conditions which must have also existed in simple one room homes in East Anglia in the 17th and 18th centuries.*

fire, with a pot or cauldron hanging from a hook above it. There would have been no ceiling, just the underside of the roof timbers and thatch, with one or two living rooms laid out in a row. These medieval and Tudor cottages would have been basic but not necessarily spartan. There would have been the trappings of their work, a few pieces of furniture like a table, and some benches or stools, and as some would have housed livestock inside their home the smell would have been significant.

The major change in the interior of a cottage came through the adoption of a fireplace and chimney which was becoming common in cottages by the end of the 17th century. This permitted an upper floor to be inserted, which might be just a gallery at one end with a ladder to access it, or a complete floor with stairs tucked in beside the fireplace. With families now sleeping upstairs there was more room below, however during the 18th century, cottage dwellers increasingly had to supplement their incomes by undertaking a trade or craft like spinning or weaving so the equipment to carry this out would have quickly filled any space back up again. Furniture would have been limited although they might now have a few chairs, built-in cupboards and a chest for their belongings.

In the Victorian period there was greater variety of housing stock for the poor, depending on where they lived. Some were tenants in well-built estate cottages, others moved to a new two-up-two-down terrace, while others were still stuck in one room hovels. The best would have had a brick floor, painted walls, a plaster ceiling and a cooking stove in the fireplace. If they had two downstairs rooms they may have reserved one as a parlour, a room originally for the better off to put their feet up at night and have a chat with the family, but now aspired to by the working classes who reserved it for Sundays and special occasions (parlour is derived from the Latin verb 'parlare' meaning to speak). Upstairs there would be a couple of bedrooms with wooden or metal bedsteads and a washbasin. If there was a small fireplace in one of the bedrooms it would only have been lit for someone infirm or ill.

For the less wealthy, floors would have been beaten earth, walls would have been rough with just a lime or colour wash coating, ceilings the underside of the floor above, and there would have been a simple grate and brick oven in the fireplace. Although some would have had first-floor sleeping accommodation there were still many using box beds against a wall in their one room.

With lower aspirations and a lifestyle which meant they spent little time at home these conditions may have been accepted by many as the norm. Perhaps surprisingly, many of these poorly built and cramped homes survived well into the 20th century. It was only as concerns about the health of the working classes were raised, and local councils began taking steps to provide better housing in the 1920s, that the situation began to improve. Today, with the lowest quality cottages gone and the better 18th and 19th-century examples mostly modernised, it is hard

to believe that in nearly every village in East Anglia people were living in these conditions only a few generations ago.

Fireplaces

The fireplace, the heart of the home, would have originally been quite a spacious area with a roof supported by a beam or brick arch. There would have been a simple iron grate in which wood or peat would have been burnt, and a small opening to one side for a bread oven. A hook and perhaps an

FIG 4.4: *Even in the 20th century many cottage dwellers with limited resources may have lived in a basic room as shown here.*

■ Inventories

Inventories from wills, and literature from the 18th and 19th centuries, can reveal much about the interior of cottages from the period. Furniture was usually limited to a small table, a few stools or chairs, a chest or cupboard and a bedstead. Other pieces which might be expected like dressers are less frequently mentioned. Most had a hook, known in Norfolk as a hake, which was used to hang pots over the fire until cooking stoves became more common in the late 19th century. Agricultural tools and equipment for a cottage trade were also found. Other items included earthenware pots, occasional pieces of pewter, glass bottles, window hangings, blankets and a few sheets. This meagre collection was usually better than that accumulated by earlier generations and a single-room cottage must have seemed quite cluttered.

iron crane would have held pots in which basic meals like stew, soup and porridge could be cooked, and a kettle for brewing tea which became available to the poor in the late 18th century. A large inglenook fireplace would give sufficient room for a simple bench at one side while a small cupboard built into the wall close by could be used for storing ingredients as the heat would have kept it dry. It was not until the late Victorian period when coal became more widely available that cast-iron cooking stoves and small ranges with a chamber for boiling water and an oven to one side were found in cottages. It was common for old fireplaces to be reduced in size to fit these new cookers

FIG 4.6: *Before village shops became common during the 19th century most food had to be grown, made or prepared at home. Bread was baked in a small brick-lined oven with a tiny door to the side of the fireplace. Early examples might have had a wooden door while most later ovens had a simple iron door (top). Sometimes ovens were added to the side of the building, creating a distinctive round bulge on the outside of the wall, although this is not common in East Anglia (bottom). These ovens became redundant when stoves and modern cookers were introduced but the arched or square opening can often still be found to the side of an old fireplace.*

FIG 4.5: *It was not until the late 19th century that simple cast-iron stoves or range cookers were found in cottages. This example has an oven to the right and a water tank to the left of the fire, with hotplates on the top. Despite their appeal they were hard to control and constantly needed cleaning.*

or more modern gas and electric heaters, so it can be fascinating to open these back up when carrying out renovations.

Floors

Before the 19th century the ground floor of most cottages in this region would have been earth. This most simple of surfaces could be just the bare ground, but usually it was enhanced by digging or raking over the surface and adding material like clay, chalk, brick dust, ash and even bulls' blood. This was then beaten or rammed down to create a reasonably smooth and hard surface. Straw could have been spread over the surface to collect the daily dirt and animal waste. Brick floors were desirable and could be found in some buildings from the late 17th century, but it was only in estate cottages and later Victorian terraces where they were common. Tiles and stone floors were

rare in labourers' homes but might be found where they could be made locally.

■ **'Water, water, everywhere, nor any drop to drink.'**
Despite being surrounded by rivers, streams and the Broads, cottage dwellers in the past would not normally have drunk fresh water. Water was used for cooking, washing and for animals, and it would have been collected from a local stream or the village pump. Sometimes, water was collected from the roof in butts while the more fortunate had a well in the garden. Beer was the staple drink of the poor in the past, weak brews were drunk throughout the day and stronger ones on special occasions. Tea became popular from the late 18th century, although the leaves which were sold to the poor were usually second-hand, having been first used by richer folk. The brewing and boiling process not only made for a tastier drop but also removed most of the harmful elements from the water which was usually contaminated by the effluence seeping into water courses, or thrown directly into it. It was not until the late 19th century that the link between disease and contaminated water was made, and many villages had to wait until the 20th century before water towers were erected, providing a reliable fresh water supply via a tap in their cottage.

FIG 4.7: *In most small cottages there would not have been a separate kitchen but a single living room in which all the meals were cooked, as in this example of a fisherman's cottage.*

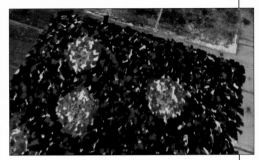

FIG 4.9: *Simple rag rugs were made by some to cheer up the floor. Old canvas bags or sacks were an alternative, especially in front of the hearth to catch sparks and cinders.*

FIG 4.8: *A cottage floor lined with bricks and tiles showing the variety of colours which are found in this region. Exposing an original surface can also show where old walls once stood within a house before modern changes.*

Upper floors were sometimes made by laying laths (thin strips of wood), sticks or reeds over the beams and covering them with a plaster mix. Floorboards could be found in the better class of village home but were not standard in a simple cottage until the 19th century.

■ The breathable cottage

Solid floors were intended to allow moisture from the ground to pass through them. Any dampness then evaporated as air flowed through the original draughty cottage. In recent times, cottages have been sealed and insulated, and fitted with carpets that restrict the way in which solid floors work. Many have also had their beaten earth or brick floors ripped up and replaced with solid concrete and a damp-proof membrane. This often causes a new problem as moisture, which formerly evaporated away, is now drawn up into the walls. Rising damp can affect the stability of the walls especially if they are of earth or clay lump. There are ways of avoiding problems where these solid floors still exist. Rugs without rubber backings allow the floor to breath and freestanding furniture with legs or castors allows air to pass below. Good ventilation, through trickle vents in double-glazed windows for example, allows air to circulate. If the floor is in such poor condition it needs to be replaced then a new system using natural hydraulic lime binders can be used which allows the floor to breathe while the aggregates included in the mix improve its insulating properties.

FIG 4.10: *A photograph showing the thin laths and plaster of a ceiling in a ruined cottage.*

Ceilings

The ceiling in many rooms was little more than the underside of the floor above, perhaps with a coat of lime wash while the bedroom could have been opened to the rafters. In 18th and 19th-century cottages a ceiling is more likely to have been fitted. These were made by nailing wooden laths across the joists and spreading a plaster mix over the slatted surface, forced in so it spread into the gaps to get a key. Plasterboard became available after the Second World War and has replaced many of these traditional ceilings.

Walls

The inner walls of a cottage would have received little more than the same coat of lime or colour wash applied to the exterior. Paintings and early photographs often show these plain white or cream walls in a rough or crumbling state, with little sign that any attempt was made by landlords to repair or decorate them. In some better properties a finer surface might be found. Paintings or drawings are sometimes uncovered on the walls of Tudor and Elizabethan houses, wooden square panelling was a quality finish in the late 16th and 17th century (much copied in the Victorian period) while a fine plastered wall would be expected in an 18th or 19th-century house. Wallpapers became affordable in the 19th century and were found in the better class of cottage. Stencilling was used elsewhere as a cheaper way of achieving a similar effect.

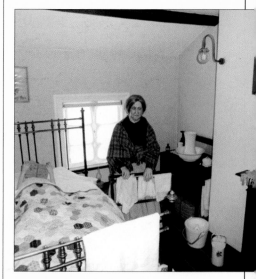

FIG 4.11: *Bedrooms would have been little more than a plain tent-like space with a simple bedstead, a crude mattress and perhaps a washstand in the corner. This photograph shows how restricted the space would have been. It was not unusual to find numerous children crammed into a bed this size sleeping top to tail.*

■ The modern cottage interior

Unlike the exterior, where an authentic appearance is desirable, and necessary for a listed building, there is more freedom with the interior. Although in the oldest properties certain original features might need to be retained (check with your local authority) the owner usually has a free hand in choosing the colour, layout and fittings. A labourer's cottage had plain interiors with few of the furnishings and fittings we now think of as essential, so it would seem better to create an appropriate style rather than trying to replicate authentic cottage rooms. Permanent changes like knocking out a wall should be carefully thought about but the style of furniture and fabrics used is very much down to personal taste.

In the kitchen, built-in furniture with long runs of worktops are convenient but don't always suit these properties. Try confining them to the sink and cooker run and using some freestanding pieces. Wall units can be a problem with low ceilings and can close a room in. It can be tempting to put new cookers in an old fireplace, but be warned you can bang your head as the space is often too low and it can make extraction difficult (fumes cannot be ducted up the chimney).

Heating a cottage can be a problem where gas is not available. Wood burners are effective and look the part but make sure they are fitted correctly with chimney liners (see p 35). Electric heating is more expensive to run but with modern storage heaters and digital remote controls they are more efficient than in the past and may suit those who do not live permanently in their cottage. Heating by oil or gas cylinders can be more effective but there is the problem of having tanks to hide, and they have higher installation and maintenance costs.

Furniture with plain or simple designs are appropriate, but do not be afraid to mix them up with a few pieces in different woods or styles, the original cottage would have contained a mix of old hand-me-downs and second-hand pieces. The current fashion is to expose natural materials. Old timber beams, stone walls and rustic brickwork are shown off and the marks, sockets and old holes found in them can be fascinating details. Avoid using oil-based paint or vinyl wallpaper on walls, water-based paints are now widely available and allow the walls to breathe. It is also a good idea to make sure that furniture or kitchen units are not tight up against an old solid wall. Try pulling them away a bit to allow air to pass behind, or reposition them on an internal dividing wall. This should help reduce any problems with mould and damp.

CHAPTER 5

The Cottage Garden
Roses, Hollyhocks and Lavender

FIG 5.1: *The informal and unpretentious arrangement of colourful flowers and climbers adds a distinctive charm and completes the image of an old cottage.*

The cottage garden we are familiar with today is a relatively modern creation. The seemingly haphazard arrangement of colourful flowers, climbers and herbs packed into beds developed in the late 19th century. Today, at its best, it is a skilled art form designed for visual impact and traditional appearance. The real gardens which would have surrounded the cottages of most village labourers up into the early 20th century were a vital source for the sustenance of the family. They produced not only vegetables, fruits and space to keep livestock but also medicines, fragrances and useful materials. It was a working plot more akin to an allotment than the beautiful floral creations that we see today.

Early cottage gardens

The cottager labourer would have used the plot immediately around his home as part of his allocation of land for growing crops and keeping livestock to feed his family. There would have been wooden outbuildings for storage or animals and there may have been a well. Pigs, hens and geese would have been common, a cow was too expensive for many labourers until the more prosperous times of the 16th

■ Boundaries

The cottage plot would have been surrounded by either simple wooden fencing or by hedging plants. Hawthorn, holly, privet and elderberry were useful not just because they formed a barrier which could keep wandering livestock off the precious crops, but they could also provide flowers and fruit for drinks and ointments, or timber which could be made into poles or small wooden implements. More elaborate picket fencing and low walls could be found around estate cottages and later 19th-century houses. If a substantial old wall surrounds a cottage today it might be an indication that either the property was once more important and has been divided or reduced in size at a later date, or that it once stood next to an important building. Crinkle-crankle walls which wind in an out are a notable feature of Suffolk and tend to date from the 18th century.

FIG 5.2: *A traditional cottage garden as it may have appeared in the early 20th century. For many it was a working space with livestock, vegetables, fruit trees and sheds.*

century, and a horse was a rarity until much later. They would have grown vegetables, including turnips, onions, cabbages, leeks, peas and broad beans and there may have also been a few fruit trees like apple, pear, and cherry, and raspberries or gooseberries. Flowers like primroses, violets, and calendulas, and herbs including sage, parsley, thyme, and lavender would have been planted in small spaces, but only because they were useful around the home rather than for their appearance. The varieties would have been limited by the soil type in the garden.

During the 18th and early 19th centuries the cottage garden began to change. Keeping a few pigs and hens and growing fruit and vegetables were still the priority, but now there was more emphasis on growing herbs and flowers, especially at the front. Some were valued for their sweet scent, others were grown for cooking, or for making dyes. Medicines were also made from plants grown in the cottage garden. The range of vegetables increased with, for example, potatoes becoming common in East Anglia from the late 18th century. More exotic

FIG 5.3: *Outbuildings down the side of a cottage or scattered around the plot can be of interest. The simple wooden structures used to store tools or keep livestock will rarely survive but more substantial brick or stone buildings might indicate that a trade was carried out on the site. The size, form and details of the structure might help establish if a carpenter or blacksmith worked there. Perhaps it was stabling for an inn, or was used to store boats and equipment for fishermen, or for those working the Fens and Broads. Old maps, photographs and trade directories can often help establish if a business was being carried out on the site.*

■ Traditional cottage garden plants

Despite not having access to a wide variety of plants there was still a good selection which the cottage dweller could have made use of. Records from as far back as the 16th century give us some clues as to what was being grown. Flowers included lavender, sweet william, primrose, violet, hollyhock, Madonna lily, corn marigold, love-lies-bleeding, and calendula. Thyme, sage, catmint, lungwort, parsley, borage, chervil, marjoram, and bergamot were some of the commonly grown herbs. Vegetables, which were grown to feed livestock and to add substance or flavour to simple meals like pottage, included onions, leeks, cabbage, broad beans, marrowfat peas, turnips, carrots and garlic. Apples, pears, plums, cherries, gooseberries and strawberries were also common. There are records that hops were widely grown in the past, after the main beer and ale producers, the monasteries, were dissolved.

FIG 5.4: *Unlike cottages which leave their history in brick, stone and timber, the garden which surrounds it leaves no such footprint. Most of what we know of their former appearance is gleaned from snippets of literature which can be hard to interpret. It is dangerous to assume that all cottage gardens developed along similar lines, just as today, the use of the garden would have depended on the individual living there. Those living in an estate village may have had a permanent garden which they were encouraged to maintain, others with a more transient lifestyle would have planted just what they needed in the short term. We can be more certain of the development of cottage gardens from the 19th century as photographs, newspapers and paintings create a more accurate picture, like this example by Helen Allingham (1885-1926).*

plants might have also found their way into the cottage garden, some from the wild but others perhaps being passed on from the head gardener of a country estate to those in the village. For the first time, flower beds and rustic walls were being used for plants which were grown purely for their appearance.

The modern cottage garden

Although romanticised images of tumbledown cottages surrounded by richly coloured flower beds and climbing plants inspired architects and gardeners alike from the late Victorian period, the informal garden with simple, hardy plants has many of its roots in the earlier estates of the rich. Some had been experimenting with this new approach for decades, and leading gardeners like Gertrude Jekyll created new wildflower gardens around some of the leading Arts and Crafts houses of the late 19th century. In contrast to the flat carpet bedding of brightly coloured annuals and the exotic foreign shrubs and trees which surrounded many large Victorian houses this new, more casual approach mixed domestic flowers, herbs and vegetables together in tightly packed beds with a carefully planned structure to form an artistic creation.

Nature and the gardener created the design in tandem. One of the most influential gardeners and writers who promoted the planting of wildflowers was William Robinson. He differed from his contemporaries by advocating a less planned approach, and helped establish the cottage garden with its simple layout of wildflowers and minimal interference from the gardener. The overall effect was of rustic charm, a homely scale, and tightly packed spaces with colours which seem to have been casually thrown together.

While these ideas permeated through the middle classes most village gardens remained practical spaces with vegetables, fruits and livestock grown to feed the family. However, there was usually a small space at the front where flowers could be grown and sometimes sold at the garden gate. The situation improved for many as allotments were established so that people could grow their own vegetables and keep livestock, freeing the garden around the

■ Gertrude Jekyll and William Robinson

The two most influential personalities who helped establish the modern concept of the cottage garden were Gertrude Jekyll (1843-1932) and William Robinson (1838-1935). From the 1870s they promoted a completely different approach to gardening using wildflowers and naturalistic planting, in line with many of the ideals of the Arts and Crafts movement. Flowers, herbs and vegetables could be planted together to create simple and informal beds, with climbers spreading over rustic garden features, and ground creeping plants breaking the borders with paths. Gertrude Jekyll (whose family is thought to have given Robert Louis Stevenson the name for his book *The Strange Case of Dr Jekyll and Mr Hyde*) had originally been an artist but turned to gardening after her eyesight began to fail. Her planting surrounded the creations of leading architects like Sir Edwin Lutyens. Her gardens were planned with a painter's eye for colour and texture. She was not only skilled in planting but also had a love of all plants and worked hard for their preservation. She wrote over 15 books, the most notable being *Colour in the Flower Garden* (1908).

William Robinson always preferred a more simple and homely creation, saying of the cottage garden that, 'it is the absence of any pretentious plan, which lets the flowers tell their story to the heart'. He is credited with introducing the herbaceous or mixed border, with native plants and hardy perennials tightly packed in, with no soil visible, and also with the use of alpine plants in rock gardens. In contrast to geometric carpet bedding he advocated wild flowers and naturalistic planting. Jekyll once said of her lifelong friend that, 'It is mainly owing to his unremitting labours that a clear knowledge of the world of hardy-plant beauty is now placed within easy reach of all who care to acquire it.'

■ Soil

There is a great variety in soil types which cover the underlying bedrock across East Anglia (see FIG 2.2). Many are quite fertile and there are areas in the north and west of Norfolk where there can be many different soils within a small area. Clays are widespread across the central part of the region, with sandy soils found around the coast and along the western edge in areas like Breckland. A good growing soil, or loam, is formed where there are even percentages of clay, sand and silts. Where one of these dominates there usually has to be some compromise in the plants grown. Feeling the texture between your fingers helps establish your soil type, but also see what neighbours grow to help work out what will be a success in your garden. Check the acidity of the soil as certain plants struggle if the pH is too high or low. Simple meters and more accurate testing kits are available from garden centres. Older cottage gardens may have been worked for centuries, and over the years treatment with compost, silts from flooding and manure from livestock will have enriched the soil. If you find the soil restricts the growing of a favourite plant you can use containers and raised beds in which the soil and compost can be controlled. Cranfield University have catalogued soil types across the country. You can find out more on soil in a specific location at www.landis.org.uk.

FIG 5.5: *Modern cottage gardens are colourful, rustic spaces with tightly packed flower beds that are richly varied and scented. Many prefer to co-ordinate colours and plan the structure, while others have a more random approach and see how things develop. Flowers, vegetables and herbs grow among each other in these small plots.*

FIG 5.6: *Fencing, arches, seats and other structural pieces around a cottage garden should be modest in size and simple in design to fit in with the cottage feel. William Robinson noted that 'One lesson of these little gardens, that are so pretty, is that one can get good effects from simple materials'. Fancy ironwork, stone statues and sundials are often found but would be more at home in a manor house garden than that of a labourer. Paling fences (left) and wicket gates are the most distinctive way of surrounding a plot and they allow plants to grow between them. Today owners might prefer more privacy so a tall hedge or fence panels can be used. These also make a good background for colourful flowers. Rustic poles made from fallen local wood can be used to make garden structures which can be left in their natural finish or painted.*

cottage for more colourful displays of plants. It was only during the 20th century, when the number of local shops supplying food increased and cottages owners had more leisure time, that the ideas of naturalistic planting and irregular design were applied to the entire garden.

Cottage garden plants

There is a huge choice of flowers, herbs, shrubs and vegetables which you can grow in a modern cottage garden. Old fashioned or native plants are always popular but there are many modern and imported variants which will add structure and are hardy. The soil type, aspect and exposure to wind and frost will have to be considered but much of the fun is in trying something out, if it does not work you can always soak the roots and move it elsewhere.

Plants are best arranged in beds with the tallest at the back and lowest at the front. Try grouping together plants with contrasting height, spread and form, and grow plain foliage between flowers to help avoid any colour clashes. Make any improvements to the soil and remove weeds before you start planting. Apart from adding light doses of fertiliser in poorer soils and mulching through the winter, maintenance should be low.

The most distinctive plant of the cottage garden is the rose, traditional types with a strong fragrance and lush foliage are the most suitable. Try Rosa gallica, Rosa centifolia, Rosa rugosa 'Rubra' and English Roses by David Austin. Climbers draped over arches or scaling the walls are also characteristic especially clematis and honeysuckle. Clematis armandii, Clematis flammula, and Lonicera periclymenum are good examples. Traditional cottage garden herbs and vegetables are still grown but others are now appreciated for their appearance like Cardoon, Jerusalem artichoke, squashes, climbing beans, and coloured lettuces. Small fruit trees are still popular, as are shrubs like dogwood and hazel.

Some plants are good at breaking up beds of colourful flowers and have interest in their leaves and structure, heucheras are good examples. Others are useful in attracting butterflies and bees, for instance buddleia, calendula, comfrey, lavender, catmint, marjoram, bergamot and borage. Wildflowers like meadow cranesbill, red campion, lady's smock and celandine are also popular. The largest group of plants in a cottage garden however are annuals and perennials. These include pansy, sweet william, marigold, lily, daisy, crocus, delphinium, dianthus, foxglove, hollyhock, geranium, Jerusalem cross, cowslip, euphorbia, lavender, evening primrose, and lily of the valley. To help narrow down this bewildering choice there are many very good books and websites which can recommend suitable flowers. The Royal Horticultural Societies website is particularly useful as you can filter the plants for soil, sunlight and garden type. (www.rhs.org.uk/plants).

FIG 5.7: *Examples of plants found in East Anglian cottage gardens.*

Places to Visit

Unlike larger houses there are only a handful of old cottages which are open to the public. Most of these are within a country estate or local museum and not all show the interiors as they originally would have appeared. Places you can visit, in this region and further afield, are listed below.

The Museum of East Anglian Life
Iliffe Way Stowmarket Suffolk
IP14 1DL
01449 612229
www.eastanglianlife.org.uk
This large museum contains a number of cottages and exhibits which show many aspects of rural life from the past.

Cromer Museum
Tucker St Cromer Norfolk NR27 9HB
01263 513543
www.museums.norfolk.gov.uk
A late 19th-century fishermen's terrace has been restored within this small and fascinating museum.

Burwell Museum of Fen Edge Village Life
Mill Close Burwell Cambridge
CB25 0HL
01638 605544
www.burwellmuseum.org.uk
This museum, with its notable windmill, tells the story of village life in the Fens and contains displays of building materials and various interiors.

Weald & Downland Open Air Museum
Town Lane Singleton nr Chichester
West Sussex PO18 0EU
01243 811363
www.wealddown.co.uk
Although not in East Anglia, this is simply the finest collection of rural houses and cottages in the country and the best place to see what conditions were really like for cottage dwellers in the past.

If you would like to experience life in an East Anglian cottage for yourself then a good way to do so is to rent one for a holiday. There are many cottage holiday companies with hundreds of properties from which to choose. There are also some historic

Cromer Museum

cottages in the care of national bodies which can be rented. Try the Landmark Trust at **www.landmarktrust.org.uk** and the National Trust at **www.nationaltrustcottages.co.uk.**

Private cottages and their gardens are easier to see when villages have open garden events. These can be found in the local press or are listed on www.opengardens.co.uk

One of the most inspirational places to visit is Barnsdale, created by the late Geoff Hamilton for the BBC's *Gardeners' World*.
Barnsdale Gardens
The Ave Exton Oakham Rutland LE15 8AH
01572 813200
www.barnsdalegardens.co.uk

For those who like to wander around beautiful villages and admire the distinctive cottages in their setting, here is a list of some of the best places to visit. If you cannot go there in person, you could always enter the postcode into Google Maps and take a virtual tour.

Thornham Norfolk PE36 6LY (also **Brancaster Staithe**). The linear villages which spread along the Cromer to Hunstanton road (A149) contain a wide variety of cottages and back onto the stunning beaches of the Norfolk coast. Thornham, where there are some clunch-built cottages, is perhaps the best example.

Burnham Market
Norfolk PE31 6LY (also **Burnham Overy Town**). Originally this was a busy little town but is now of village proportions with many excellent buildings around the green. Well worth taking a detour to explore.

Blakeney
Norfolk NR25 7NX (also **Cley Next The Sea**). This old port has good examples of coastal cottages, most of which are made from or faced with local pebbles.

Blakeney

New Houghton
Norfolk PE31 6UE (also **Hillington**). If visiting Houghton Hall, take a moment to see this row of white painted semi-detached estate cottages. They were built in the 18th century when the original village was moved to make way for a new park. There

New Houghton

are also good examples of carstone
cottages to the south-west along the
A148 in Hillington.

Stokesby
Norfolk NR29 3EX. There are a
number of picturesque villages around
the Broads. Stokesby is one of the best
examples with a good mix of cottages.
There is also a windmill and cottage
about half a mile west along the
river Bure.

Somerleyton
Suffolk NR32 5PU. An excellent estate
village with picturesque cottages
around the green and along The Street.

New Buckenham
Norfolk NR16 2AF (also **Banham and
Kenninghall**). An old town built in the
shadow of the Norman castle and now
with the feel of a village untouched by
time. Many excellent houses and
cottages with other good examples to
the south-west in Banham and
Kenninghall.

Pulham Market
Norfolk IP21 4SU (also **Pulham St
Mary** and **Starston**). A number of
attractive thatched cottages around the
green and lanes.

Methwold
Norfolk IP26 4NT (also **Feltwell,
Stoke Ferry** and **Wereham**). A good
example of a Fens village with a
number of notable buildings. Wereham
to the north-east, just off the A134, is
very picturesque.

Walberswick
Suffolk IP18 6UA (also **Westleton**).
A popular setting opposite the
attractive seaside town of Southwold.
Many good houses and cottages in
both and they are linked by a ferry.
Walk up Palmers Lane by the church.
Westleton to the south has many good
cottages especially around the green.

Peasenhall
Suffolk IP17 2JQ (also **Yoxford**). A
good example of an East Anglian
linear village with lanes either side of a
central stream flanked by cottages.
Also some fine buildings in Yoxford.

Debenham
Suffolk IP14 6QJ. Attractive old
houses and cottages around this old
market town whose back lanes are
also worth exploring. There are good
buildings to the north in Eye, and
south in Coddenham.

Brent Eleigh
Suffolk CO10 9NS (also **Monks Eleigh**
and **Chelsworth**). One in a series of
attractive villages along the A1141.
This is notable for its colourful
cottages around the triangular green.
Lavenham is also just to the east and
is always worth a visit to see its

Brent Eleigh

wonderful collection of timber-framed buildings.

Kersey
Suffolk IP7 6DY. One of the finest villages in the region with houses and cottages flanking the lane either side of its much photographed ford.

Kersey

Nayland
Suffolk CO6 4JE (also **Stoke-by-Nayland**). Another excellent village in an area which benefitted from the wool trade. Notable timber-framed cottages and buildings around the mill and Birch Street.

Cavendish
Suffolk CO10 8AZ (also **Clare**). Another attractive Suffolk village, especially around the green with its pink thatched cottages. There are some good cottages around the church in Clare.

Linton
Cambs CB21 4HS (also **Great Chesterford** and **Little Chesterford**, Essex). Just over the border is this exceptional village with cottages amidst the fine houses lining the old main road. The Chesterfords to the south-west are more rural and contain many fine cottages.

Finchingfield
Essex CM7 4JX. One of the most photographed villages in the country. There are many attractive cottages set around the green and back lanes.

Websites
The following websites may be useful if you are researching a specific cottage or seeking advice about maintenance and restoration.
www.britishlistedbuildings.co.uk
www.heritagegateway.org.uk
www.heritage.norfolk.gov.uk
www.english-heritage.org.uk/ professional
www.spab.org.uk
www.buildingconservation.com
www.periodproperty.co.uk
www.climatechangeandyourhome. org.uk
www.thatchingadvisoryservices.co.uk
www.eartha.org.uk (buildings with earth)
www.thecottagegardensociety.org.uk
www.rhs.org.uk/advise

Books
The Buildings of England series begun by **Nikolaus Pevsner** is a useful source of information about architectural styles in the individual counties.
R.W. Brunskill is a leading authority on vernacular architecture and his books, including *Houses and Cottages of Britain*, are always informative. The beautifully illustrated books by **Matthew Rice** including *Building Norfolk* are also of note. Those wanting to create a cottage garden could refer to **Geoff Hamilton's** *Cottage Gardens*.

Glossary

AXIAL:	A feature or plan along the axis of a house.
BALUSTER:	A plain or decorated post supporting a stair rail.
BARGEBOARD:	External diagonal boards on a gable end that protect the ends of a sloping roof. They are often decorated (many are Victorian in date).
BAULK:	A regional term for a large timber beam.
BAY:	A vertical division of a house between trusses, sometimes with a column of windows.
BAY WINDOW:	A window projecting from the facade of a house up one or more storeys and usually resting on the ground.
BEAM:	A large horizontal timber.
BOND/BONDING:	The pattern in which bricks are laid with different arrangements of headers and stretchers to ensure the strength of the structure.
BRESSUMMER:	A term which can refer to a number of different horizontal beams but especially the one on the bottom of the upper wall of a jettied building.
BRIDGING BEAM:	A large beam running down the centre of the ceiling into which the joists are fixed (also known as a summer). It usually has chamfered or moulded lower edges.
BUTTRESS:	A vertical support angled up against a wall. Examples from the Arts and Crafts period tend to have a steep slope down their full height.
CAMES:	Lead work which holds the small panes of glass in a window.
CASEMENT WINDOW:	A window which is hinged along one side.
CAST IRON:	A brittle metal formed in moulds, whereas wrought iron is pliable and can be forged into decorative patterns.
CHIMNEYPIECE:	An internal fireplace surround.
COBBLE:	A water-rounded stone, larger than a pebble.
COURSE:	A single horizontal layer of bricks or stones in a wall.
DAMP-PROOF MEMBRANE:	A waterproof barrier incorporated within walls and ground floors to stop rising damp penetrating the structure above. Introduced in the late Victorian period.
DIAPER:	A diamond pattern formed in walls by different coloured bricks.

DORMER WINDOW: An upright window set in the angle of the roof and casting light into the upper rooms.

DUTCH GABLES: A gable with concave and convex quadrants, and triangles and right angles.

EAVES: The section of the roof timbers under the tiles, slates or thatch where they project beyond the wall.

FACADE: The main vertical face of the house.

FINIAL: An ornamental piece on top of a railing or at the end of a roof ridge.

FLUE: The duct for smoke from the fireplace up into the chimney.

FLUSHWORK: Squared, knapped flint, set flush with the face of dressed stone.

GABLE: The pointed upper section of wall at the end of a pitched roof.

GALLETS/GALLETING: Flint chips or small stones set in mortar joints for decoration.

GLAZING BARS: The wooden or metal divisions of a window which support the panes.

GOTHIC: Medieval architecture based around the pointed arch.

GOTHIC REVIVAL: The rediscovery of Gothic architecture which was championed by Pugin and Ruskin and dominated building from the 1850s to 1870s.

HALF-TIMBERING: Another term for timber-framed construction. In some cases used to refer to a building with a stone or brick lower storey and a timber-framed upper.

HANGING TILES: Clay tiles hung vertically off thin strips of wood to cover walls.

HEADER: The short end of a brick seen in the face of a wall. Stretchers are the long sides.

HEARTH: The stone or brick base of a fireplace.

HERRINGBONE: Brickwork laid in a zigzag pattern.

HIPPED ROOF: A roof with a slope on all four sides.

HOOD MOULD: Moulding in stone or brick over a window or door to throw off rainwater.

INGLENOOK: A wide recessed space for a fire often with seating to the sides.

JAMB: The side of an opening for a door or window.

JETTY: The projection of an upper storey of a timber-framed building.

JOISTS: Timber, concrete or steel beams which support a floor.

KNAP: To work flint by striking it to make a more regular shape or to make a flat surface on one or more sides.

LACING COURSE: Intermittent horizontal bands of bricks used to level up and tie the faces of a wall together.

LINTEL: A flat beam above a door or window to bear the load of the wall above.

LOAD BEARING: A wall which has to support a load, usually referring to an internal wall which helps support an upper storey or the roof timbers.

MANSARD ROOF: A roof formed from two slopes at different angles which allow more space for a room within.

MORTAR: Used to fill in gaps between stones and bricks. It evens out the load and weatherproofs the wall as well as helping to hold the pieces in place. Traditionally it was made using lime but modern mortars are cement based.

MOULDING: A projecting strip of wood, stone or plaster on a wall, or around an opening, which has a moulded profile.

MULLION: The vertical member dividing up a window.

ORIEL: A prominent projecting window from an upper storey.

PANELLING: Wooden lining of interior walls with vertical muntins and horizontal rails framing the panels.

PANTILES: Wavy or roughly 'S'-shaped clay roof tiles.

PARGETTING: A raised or incised pattern formed in plaster on an external wall.

PEBBLEDASH: Render with small pebbles and stones thrown against it before it dries.

PITCH: The angle at which a roof slopes. A plain sloping roof with two sides is called a pitched roof.

PLINTH: A low stone or brick base under a timber-framed or mud wall building.

POST: A large vertical load-bearing timber.

PURLIN: A horizontal timber beam which runs along the pitch of a roof.

QUOIN: The cornerstones at the external junction of two walls.

RAFTERS: Timbers which are set in a row along the slope of the roof with laths running horizontally across their upper surface onto which the tiles are fixed.

RAIL: A lesser horizontal timber between main posts and beams.

RENDER: A protective covering for a wall made from two or three layers of plaster or cement.

REVEAL: The sides of a recess in a wall for a window or door.

RIDGE: The top section or capping of a roof.

ROUGHCAST: A render with small stones mixed in to give a rough texture when dried.

SASH WINDOW: A window with two separate sashes which slide vertically, or horizontally on shorter Yorkshire sash windows.

SCREED:	A mix of sand and cement used to form the top layer of a ground floor.
SILL:	The horizontal timber beam at the bottom of the wall or under a window.
STRAPWORK:	Flat bands of wood or plaster which form decorative and geometric patterns.
STRETCHER:	The long side of a brick seen in the face of a wall. Headers are the short ends.
STRING COURSE:	A horizontal flat band or moulding running across a facade.
STUD:	A lesser vertical timber between main posts and beams.
TERRACOTTA:	Fine clay moulded into decorative pieces and fired. It is usually left unglazed on Arts and Crafts buildings.
TRANSOM:	A horizontal bar above a window.
VERNACULAR:	Buildings made from local materials in the regional style using methods of construction passed down within a particular area to make domestic and functional structures.
VOUSSOIR:	A tapered stone or brick used to make an arch.
WAINSCOT:	Timber lining of the lower part of a wall.
WALL PLATE:	The main horizontal timber which runs along the top of the wall and under the eaves.
WEATHERBOARDING:	Overlapping horizontal planks used to protect timber-framed structures from the elements or to disguise poor quality construction.
YORKSHIRE SASH WINDOWS:	Sliding sash windows found in period farmhouses and cottages.

I hope you have enjoyed this book. If you have, and want to learn about others I've written, then please visit **www.countrysidebooks.co.uk**. My titles are available as softcover books and eBooks.

Follow **Countryside Books** on **facebook** and click 'Like' for the latest new titles and competitions.

Trevor Yorke

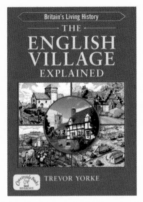

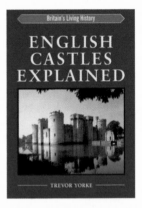

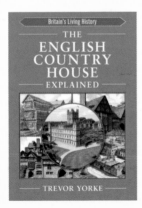

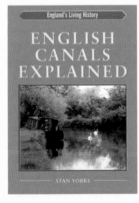

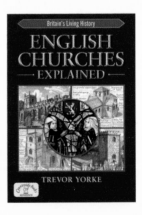